The Giraffe and Jackal Within

CW00545009

The Giraffe and Jackal WITHIN
About Nonviolent Communication

Justine Mol

translated by Dawn Mastin

uitgeverij
SWP

Original title:
Justine Mol (6e druk 2012). *De giraf en de jakhals in ons. Over
geweldloos communiceren*. Amsterdam: Uitgeverij SWP
(ISBN 978 90 8850 387 0)

The Giraffe and Jackal Within
About Nonviolent Communication
Justine Mol

ISBN 978 90 8850 373 3
NUR 847

© 2012 SWP Publishers, Amsterdam
All rights reserved. No part of this publication may be reproduced in any
form without the written permission of SWP Publishers, Amsterdam,
The Netherlands. Any person who does any unauthorised act in relation to this publication may be liable to prosecution and civil claims
for damages.

Contents

Foreword

In my work, I used to travel all around the world with a jackal and giraffe puppet. I use them in my work. I use the symbol of giraffes as a symbol for Nonviolent Communication because giraffes have the largest heart of any land animals and Nonviolent Communication is a language of the heart. I use the jackal symbol for language that disconnects us from one another and makes violence enjoyable. I have no good reason for selecting the jackal other than many of the people I work with seem to enjoy the word 'jackal' and it heightens their enjoyment of learning Nonviolent Communication.

In this book, Justine Mol has succeeded in my opinion in giving an overview of the different aspects of the "giraffe" and "jackal" in each of us in a way that heightens the learning process of Nonviolent Communication in a fun way.

Marshall Rosenberg

Introduction

'As proud as a peacock.' 'As wily as a fox.'

As human beings, we poetically attribute certain qualities to animals. We could say that animals clearly and quite one-dimensionally demonstrate certain qualities, while in our self, we are able to distinguish a combination of these qualities. At one moment, the timidity of the mouse takes centre stage, and at the next, we're as slow as snails.

Much use is made of this in many children's books, cartoon films and works of art. The associations we make with animals are often so essential that words are unnecessary. When we use animals as images, we speak a universal language with no borders.

In the Native American tradition, animals appear as totems. The symbolism represented by animals helps people to fathom the mysteries of life. We can benefit from tuning in to the qualities of an animal crossing our path and asking ourselves what it says about us, or what we can learn from it.

The founder of Nonviolent Communication, Marshall Rosenberg, chose two animals to lend power and clarity to the expression of his ideas: the jackal and the giraffe. These two represent two qualities in us: the tendencies to alienate and to connect. The jackal symbolizes the denial of fear and pain and the reaching for means such as power, aggression and manipulation in order to survive. This running away from what is really alive in us does not always happen in an aggressive or negative way. It can also take the form of telling someone how wonderful they are or by being artificially nice, which I also see as a form of manipulation.

When I climb into the skin of my jackal, I am goal-oriented. I don't see other people or myself as vulnerable, but as a means of achieving my goal. I make judgments, I apportion blame, I am demanding and authoritarian. Marshall called his children 'little jackals' when they were small. He used the word as a pet name and they loved it. Once, a woman was giving him a lift to a workshop. She asked him if he would work with her on her relationship with her husband. They had done this during previous journeys and Marshall said: "Aren't you sick of working on that jackal?" She knew immediately what he meant. He decided to introduce the word 'jackal' that evening during his workshop to see how people would respond. He imagined that no-one would know what he was talking about, but everyone turned out to know a 'jackal' personally.

Marshall then started looking for a second animal to symbolize embracing the fear and the pain: for the aspect of ourselves that is interested in what's alive and pays kind attention to it. He first came up with a duck, but that wasn't quite it. A duck was too feeble, could be savaged to death by the jackal in no time at all. It needed to be an animal that was both gentle and strong. And that's how he settled on the giraffe. When I climb into the skin of my giraffe, I have the intention of staying in connection with what's alive inside both me and in other people. I remain in the now, and look at whatever turns up with kindness. I don't sink into old patterns and misery from the past, nor do I concern myself with how to keep going, with solutions. The giraffe has a very large heart and this is why Marshall chose it to symbolize communication from the heart.

In 1998, I came across the giraffe and the jackal in Ode (an alternative news magazine on ideas for change) in an article about Nonviolent Communication by Marshall Rosenberg. In Nonviolent Communication, the object is not to win or to be right, but to listen to each other and to live with our differences. My partner, René, and I had been having a relationship for one year by that time. We had both been married before and had resolved to do things differently this time. Unfortunately, we didn't know how. So, just as before, if something was bothering us, we would give each other the blame: he got angry and I cried. I complained to my female friends and he digested in silence. Our love always won through and then we'd be fine again. But our trust in each other was continually sustaining dents and we were heading straight for a break-up.

We can truthfully say that Nonviolent Communication saved our relationship. We bought Rosenberg's book and went to a workshop. I said goodbye to my speech therapy practice and became an internationally certified trainer in Nonviolent Communication. René and I were together for 11 years. Our harmony, our pleasure at being together and our deep bond did not come of their own accord. In 2009 René and I changed our relationship into friendship.
Also in this process Nonviolent Communication supported us. When our conversations became grim, we took a time-out. We always came back to our longing for connection. We still keep practicing in accepting and respecting our differences. We take responsibility for what we feel and need. (Well, sometimes we give each other the blame first, but that doesn't last as long as it used to.) We enjoy each other's qualities and stimulate each other to use and develop them. We share a deep longing to live in wholeness and love with the earth and everyone and everything on it and with the spiritual world pervading it.

In this constant search for connection, I am supported by the giraffe and the jackal. I have a couple of hand-puppets and two sets of ears sewn onto Alice-bands that I can put on my head. At first, when the volume at which René and I were talking began to climb and the tone became fiercer, I would walk out on the conversation and retreat to my room. I'd put on my giraffe ears and listen kindly and with understanding to my jackal, full of judgments of René, and to René's jackal, judging me. I would then go back to find René and give my attention to the feelings and needs hiding behind his jackal. Sometimes I'd be back in my room with the giraffe ears on again within two minutes. Ah well, we all have to learn to walk before we can run.

I use the hand-puppets in my work too. I sometimes work with children, but usually with adults. Some of my students take these images with them into their daily lives. And then miracles happen. One woman wasn't sure whether to participate in one of my workshops. She was in the middle of a divorce and that was demanding a lot of her energy. She wasn't sure if she could handle the workshop on top of everything else. She decided to try it. After a week, I saw her again. She was so happy with her giraffe. When her husband started blaming or accusing her again, she would visualize two giraffe ears on her head. This helped her to listen more deeply to her husband, to his despair and fear, to what he longed for. She came to several more of my workshops. And – you guessed it – the divorce never took place.

Another example: during a workshop, the participants and I had imagined ourselves in the skins of the jackal and the giraffe while walking around the room. One man, who found movement exercises a great support in his learning process, told me later: "I often get really irritated at my colleague's behavior at the office. I can feel the jackal appearing inside me. My arms, shoulders and neck get tense. I pull my head down between my shoulders as if I want to hide. I look down or turn my head away. And it gets really chaotic in my head, judgments tumbling over one another. When I realize this, and decide to step out of the jackal and into the giraffe, my body relaxes. My head straightens up and my neck literally grows longer. I can look at my colleague, my breathing calms down and my heart opens. I'm really happy about this. My contact with my colleague is much better and I enjoy my work now."

So – who is to say what these two animals might be able to offer you? I have become so familiar with them that I recognize them all the time, both in myself and in others. It helps me to be aware of my state of being. And because I am aware of it, I am able to take responsibility for it. I can choose who I want to be: jackal or giraffe.

1 Introducing the Jackal and the Giraffe

In 2005, I wrote my first book, 'Growing up in Trust'. The inspiration for writing it came while I was working on a story about a meeting between a jackal and a giraffe. The story was not published at the time. I would like to start my second book with it.

An Unusual Meeting

Furious, I jump into the car and drive to the woods. I stamp along the paths and kick everything within reach of my feet. At the same time, I'm cursing my daughter's teacher (who gave her forty hours worth of homework for the summer holidays and then never even looked at it), the rewards and punishments on which our educational system is run, and yes, our whole society on which that system is based. "Don't they understand that this shatters any sense of initiative for or pleasure in learning? They haven't the first idea of how they try to pigeon-hole everything, control everything, because of their fear. They want to control everything that happens in this world..."

After a while, the anger ebbs away. There's no point. I can't change the world, even if I try. I'm an insignificant victim of the rich and powerful. Slowly, the tears begin to trickle down my cheeks. I give up. There's no use fighting. The only thing I can do is comfort my daughter and send her back to school each day, where she goes with steadily increasing reluctance.

Suddenly, I hear something in the bushes. I come to a halt and find myself looking directly into the eyes of a jackal. I'm somehow not really surprised and I look back calmly. I sense that the jackal has something to say to me. It's just like in one of my dreams. All the characters in my dreams have something to do with me. They are a part of me, manifesting outside of myself so I can observe them quietly. Does this jackal have something to do with my anger and sadness, with the thoughts which were just racing through my head?

We stand looking at each other for several moments and then the jackal slowly starts to approach me. When he is just in front of me, he lies down in the middle of the path. I look around and find what I am looking for: a tree-stump about two meters away from me. I walk over to it and sit down.

At that instant, the jackal begins to speak. "So, about time! I've been following you for years. Just like you, I think I know what needs to happen to make the world a better place. I've been trying to get your attention in all sorts of ways, but you just never see me. You probably think you can do it all on your own. You should learn some cooperation."

This last remark is, in my eyes, uncalled for. "What do you mean? If you think we can make a difference together, you could have announced your presence a bit more clearly. You could have just come and stood in front of me. I would have seen you!" My calm has vanished and my fury has returned in all its vehemence. I'm sick and tired of hearing other people tell me how I should think and what I should do.

The jackal takes on a threatening attitude and I get up from the tree-stump I'm sitting on. We may well have attacked one another at that point, had it not been for an enormous shadow passing over us at that very moment. We both halt in our tracks and look at each other distrustfully. Then simultaneously, we turn our heads in the direction of the shadow.

Standing there is a decidedly tall animal, high on its legs, and with a long neck. It's a giraffe. I am immediately sobered. Is this giraffe a part of me too? This could get interesting. I sense that this is a chance to learn all sorts of things about myself and I resolve to pay attention. The giraffe turns around and walks off into the woods on its stately legs. The jackal and I follow, curious. The giraffe leads us to a neglected tree-house and invites us to climb up into it so we can all look each other in the eye from an equal height. It's tricky, but with some huffing and puffing, the jackal and I are aloft and make ourselves as comfortable as possible. I decide to hold back so the jackal and the giraffe can converse.

The giraffe asks us what's bothering us. I remain silent. The jackal, grateful for the opportunity to vent, kicks off. "She," he says with a violent movement of his head in my direction, "has been letting people walk all over her for years! She was brought up to be a good little girl and since then, she's learned nothing. Her children used to enjoy going to school to begin with, but now, they hate it more and more by the day. And do you think that woman ever actually stands up for her children? Of course not! She has a friendly chat with a teacher every now and then. And if nothing changes, she goes around complaining at home. I've been wanting to encourage her to get tough with the school so often, but she never even sees me!"

The jackal is out of breath from talking so fast and as he gasps for air, the giraffe speaks. "Do you get frustrated at the way Justine's kids — and perhaps lots of other kids — are taught, so all the fun goes out of learning?"

"Yes, there's nothing right with the education system. They should let the kids pick what and how they want to learn. All the schools have to do is create the necessary conditions by providing an environment with all sorts of learning materials where the kids can get on with learning in peace and safety."

In a warm tone of voice, the giraffe sums up what she has heard the jackal say. "It sounds as if you have a clear image of how schools could be a paradise for children.

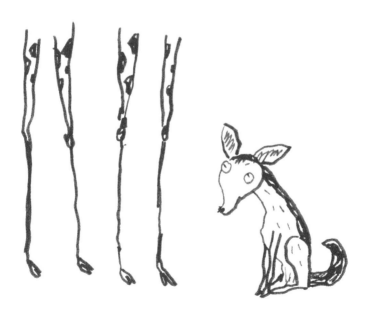

What would you expect from the teachers in a school like that?"

The jackal has thought about this too. "They should have respect for how the children are feeling and what they want, which will change from day to day according to their mood and physical condition. They should guide kids and never force them to do things. Teachers should take care of their own health and make sure they keep enjoying their work. The most important thing is that they love the children."

The giraffe is obviously enjoying the jackal's enthusiasm. "You think it's important that children's basic needs for respect and acknowledgement are met and that teachers also take care of meeting their own needs. What about setting boundaries? Would there be rules at a school like that?"

The jackal continues: "People only stick to rules if they are involved in making them. There shouldn't be any punishment. If someone doesn't stick to a rule, teachers should look at why not."

The giraffe is silent and the jackal watches her questioningly. I recognize the ideals outlined by the jackal. I hear how he uses the word 'should' and sense that he would like to shove his ideals down the throats of everyone involved in education. I'm just about to say something about this, when the giraffe beats me to it. "You know exactly how you would like the education system to be run. You feel impotent. How can you convince other people? You had pinned your hopes on Justine."

The giraffe looks deep into the jackal's eyes and the mildness with which she continues is almost palpable.

"Dearest jackal, you would like children and grown-ups to treat each other with respect at school. Is that right?" The jackal nods. "I worry when I hear you use the word 'should' a number of times. I don't think people in the field of education will want to listen to you if you come and tell them what they 'should' do. I would approach them in a different way. Shall I tell you how?"

The jackal has become curious and is eager to hear more. "How would it be to ask Justine and others to approach people working in education with understanding, respect, and compassion for what they are doing now, and to offer them the opportunity of discovering what they feel and need to make things more amenable to both themselves and the children? Let's give these people in education the opportunity of discovering and paying attention to the jackal and the giraffe in themselves. I suspect that if they freely choose to pay attention to their own and the children's feelings and needs, this will permanently change how they teach." The jackal nods again.

At almost the same moment, the jackal and the giraffe turn their heads toward me and ask, as with one voice: "Justine, will you help bring respect and compassion into child-rearing and education?"

I am elated at the question. I can put the passion behind my anger to use. I no longer have to feel powerless. I say a heart-felt 'yes' to the question and pose one of my own: "Would you help me? Will you be there if I need you? You, jackal, to help me see what's bothering me and where I get stuck? And you, giraffe, to make it clear to me what I feel and need, so I can look for the help and support I need?" The giraffe agrees immediately. The jackal says jokingly: "I'm willing, but you'll have to make an effort to see me. I'm not going to wait for years again. Next time, I'll just go for your jugular."

Before we fall out of the tree-house, fighting and squabbling, the giraffe offers us her neck to slide down. With a thud, I land in a pile of leaves. I get up and look around. I am alone again. I don't mind at all. I'm so excited about this meeting. I set off at a good pace and, as I walk to the car, the first ideas for the work awaiting me are already bubbling to the surface.

Several editions of my book 'Growing up in Trust' have already appeared. It has been translated into five languages. I give lectures and workshops about bringing up and teaching children without rewards or punishment. Following naturally from bringing children up without reward or punishment, comes living without reward or punishment. I speak about this too.

In my work as a Nonviolent Communication trainer and coach, I see parents and educators, but also people surrounded mostly by adults. I notice that the differences in the way I interact with children and with adults are receding. Adults have more life experience, but they are not always wiser. If we talk less at children and listen to them more, we gain access to their wisdom. This results in equality and mutual respect.

Most importantly, I see that developing, learning and growing do not stop when we become adults. 'Raising ourselves' is something we can continue to do until the day we die.

My field of work includes everyone who wants to grow in awareness and become conscious.

2 Marshall Rosenberg and Nonviolent Communication

Marshall Rosenberg lives in Albuquerque now. Before that he traveled all over the world with his brainchild, Nonviolent Communication. Well into his seventies, he traveled from hither to yon giving lectures, workshops and interviews. He also acted as a mediator for government leaders, married couples and everyone in between. In amongst all this, he wrote books. Wherever he went, a giraffe and a jackal traveled with him in his suitcase.

He is supported in his work by the Center for Nonviolent Communication (CNVC), which he founded in 1984 and is based in America. The aim of CNVC is to achieve a critical mass of people communicating nonviolently, leading to inner, interpersonal and organizational peace.

Nowadays, there is a world-wide network of hundreds of certified trainers. And an untraceable number of people 'living' and spreading Nonviolent Communication for whom it has become an essential aspect of the search for peace in their lives and work. It can enhance every world view and can be applied to any occupation, whether trainer, shopkeeper, manager, teacher, parent, civil servant, doctor or nurse.

There is a model for Nonviolent Communication, but the model itself is not what it's all about. It's about the intention of connecting with what's alive in your self and in the other.

If Marshall's communication model is used to get a preconceived plan carried out, little will change in our relationship with ourselves or with other people. It will just be another trick, one from a generous arsenal. But the model can also be regarded as a tool for rebuilding our inner selves, so our vision of the world and life does a complete turnabout (or however much of a turnabout is still necessary, depending on how far we have already turned).

With or without social revolution, we can try to change the world by changing the structure of society. In my opinion, such changes are doomed to failure, as individual people still continue to think in the same way. More effective would be a revolution of the human mind, an essential change in the structure and nature of our thinking.

There are undoubtedly many ways of bringing about this revolution. I have sought and found it in Nonviolent Communication. Which is why this book is about Nonviolent Communication.

I have learned to see the way a conversation progresses as being more important than its outcome. Is there mutual respect? Are we being open and authentic about our thoughts and feelings?

Whether we agree to buy this or that computer program or go on holiday to Spain or New Zealand isn't so important any more. As long as we both enjoy exploring the possibilities of whichever computer program we choose, as long as we enjoy our holidays together and come home well rested.

I think of myself as always striving for harmony and connection. I'm an avid reader and have been devouring books all my life. I look for books in which I can read how to live with myself and others in a loving way. The world is full of them. People (and therefore books too) have always told of living in unconditional love, living in the now, living in connection with others, with nature, with God and the spiritual world. They help us to develop our consciousness. It is up to us to act according to these insights, gradually establishing heaven on earth. We could say that every religion offers us the same lessons in love, just differently packaged. If we concentrate on these and other similarities between the various religions, we experience connection. If all religious people were to do this, it would mean the end of religious wars.

Indian political and spiritual leader Mahatma Gandhi who in around 1900 developed the concept of 'passive resistance' (or non-violent resistance), compares religion with a tree. If we can see only lots of branches, we tend to say there are lots of religions. If we can see the tree as a whole, we understand that there is only one religion.

Inayat Khan, an Indian musician living at around the same time, was very interested in religion. He established the Universal Worship service. During this service, seven candles are lit on an altar: six for each of the major world religions and one for all the others together. Texts are then recited from the holy books from the various religions and prayers are offered to the One God.

Nonviolent Communication goes beyond the boundaries of all religions and world views. It gives practical assistance in listening without prejudice and teaches how, while our opinions can differ widely, we can still cooperate with one another. I don't call Nonviolent Communication a method, but a *lifestyle*, because it permeates all our actions, thinking and feeling. The form into which this lifestyle has been fashioned gives me the support I need in my everyday life to live the love I have read about over the years in various books and heard about at all sorts of courses and workshops.

By now, you may be curious about this new tool for performing old and familiar tasks. I will explain the basic principles of Marshall Rosenberg's ideas overleaf. For a fuller understanding, I refer you to his books, especially 'Nonviolent Communication, a Language of Life'.

Marshall speaks of a model consisting of four elements. These elements are:
- *Observation*
- *Feelings*
- *Needs**
- *Requests*

If these elements are woven through what we say, we have a chance of being heard and of being able to hear other people. We say what is going on inside us, how we experience things, and are interested in what's going on in other people. All this is permeated with a mildness and acceptance of what is. If we speak in this way, we are speaking giraffe language.

Classic 'Giraffe' sounds like this:
"When I hear you went on a date with my boss, I feel insecure. I need safety and trust. Would you please not tell him what I've told you about my job?"

The four elements of the model are all neatly lined up: observation (you went out with my boss), feeling (insecure), need (for safety and trust) and request (would you not tell him what I told you?). However, we don't always adhere to this exact framework in practice. We may say the elements in a different order or leave one or more of them out. The important thing as far as the contact is concerned is that there is an intention to connect.

---

* This refers to universal basic needs.

I can sometimes say nothing while still being a perfect giraffe. I radiate it in my attitude, or my facial expression which shows what's in my heart. I once attended a parents' council meeting at school. Afterwards, I told another parent that I thought I hadn't contributed much. I hadn't said much. She answered: "Your participation was in being present. You sitting there listening attentively made it easier for us to arrive at insights and creative solutions."

Another example of giraffe language:
A man has done his shopping and when he arrives home, his wife sees that he hasn't got any bread. "I see there isn't any bread. I feel irritated because I'd like a nice fresh slice of bread right now and I think you forgot to buy it. I'd like to be able to trust that if someone says they'll do something for me, they will in fact do it. Could you tell me how come there's no bread?"
Let's take this example and get the elements of the model clear again.

- *Observation*: "I see there isn't any bread." This is a fact. There is no bread amongst the shopping on the kitchen counter.

- *Feeling*: "I feel irritated because I think you forgot to buy it." I say what I feel and I explain the thoughts on which the feeling is based. By doing this, I take responsibility for my feeling. If I were to say: "I feel irritated because you forgot the bread again", I would be giving you the blame for my irritation and I don't want to do that. I don't want to get into attacking and defending, I want to stay in contact.

- *Need*: "I'd like to be able to trust that if someone says they'll do something for me, they will in fact do it." I need trust and peace. If I know that something will be done, I don't have to attend to it any more and that gives me peace. (I am deliberately using the word 'someone' and not 'you', because a need always has something universal and its fulfillment never depends on one specific person performing one specific action at one specific time.)

- *Request*: "Could you tell me how come there's no bread?" With this question, I am showing my interest. I want to hear more facts so I can empathize with what's going on in the person coming home without the bread. I might otherwise ask something like: "How is it for you to hear this reaction of mine?" Here, I go directly to the other's feelings and needs in response to my reaction at there being no bread. Or I could ask: "What shall we eat now?" I have shared what's going on in me and now want to seek a solution together.

In jackal language, I might respond to the person who did the shopping like this:
"Why have you forgotten to buy bread again? I feel like you don't listen to me. Now I have to go into town myself in this lousy weather. You can clean up the kitchen in the meantime. Then at least you'll be doing something useful!" Here too, are four elements: the counterparts of the four elements of giraffe language.

The four elements of jackal language are:
- *Interpreting/judging*
- *Quasi-feeling*
- *Seeing strategies as needs*
- *Demanding*

I'll describe the elements in relation to our example.

- *Interpreting/judging*: In "Why have you forgotten to buy bread again?" I hear beside the observation (he didn't bring any bread), an interpretation (I'm assuming he forgot the bread - I don't actually know that this is true. The baker's may have been closed or perhaps he ran out of money) and a judgment (again).

- *Quasi-feeling*: To my mind, "I feel like you don't listen to me" doesn't express a feeling, but a thought (the other person doesn't listen to me). I probably have a judgment about this too and this is probably clear from my tone of voice. I may be feeling angry or sad about it, but I don't say so. So I use the word 'feel' without actually naming my feelings at all.

- *Mixing up strategies and needs*: Going into town myself to get the bread is only one way or strategy to get food. The basic need here is food, not specifically bread. If I think I need to have bread, I may feel sorry for myself or angry at the other person. I forget that there are all sorts of other ways to get food. I could for instance decide to eat some crackers or yoghurt and get some bread tomorrow. I could ask my partner to go into town again. I could borrow some bread from the neighbors. Or whatever.

- *Demanding*: "You can clean up the kitchen" is what I call a demand. It leaves no room for a response. There is another judgment in "Then at least you'll be doing something useful!" For punishment, you get to clean up the kitchen.

If we want to convince someone that we are right, we tend to weave these elements into our words. There is a fair chance that we will find ourselves entering into a discussion or even a conflict.

We communicate not only with the outside world, but with ourselves. Our jackals and giraffes also react to what we think and do ourselves. Just now I took a break from writing and wanted to eat my lunch outside and read for a bit. First I forgot my glass of milk and then I had to go back a second time for the book I wanted to read.

My jackal could have said: "You're off in the clouds again, aren't you? You are stupid. I get so sick of this. Just learn to think before you act."

My giraffe might have smiled and said: "You're still thinking about the book you're writing, aren't you? And now you'll have to make three trips – sigh. You wish you'd brought everything in one go."

The four elements of the model are not always identifiable in so many words. Let's examine this last giraffe response. I *observe* that I'm still thinking about the book I'm writing and that I make three trips back and forth. The sigh refers to a *feeling* of tiredness and discontent. The last sentence indicates that I *need* rest and that I feel empathy for the fact that, with things as they are, my rest will have to wait for a bit. By talking to myself like this, I fulfill my need for empathy and acceptance and I comply with my unspoken wish *(request)* to be kind to myself.

This was an explanation of the model on which Rosenberg's ideas are based. I do hope you won't now weigh your every word before daring to open your mouth. Remember? Intention is the most important thing. A fruitful way I have found of playing with these elements is by first listening to myself or other people and identifying the giraffe and the jackal in what is said, so the difference becomes clear.

If you try this, I recommend keeping it to yourself to begin with. If someone screams: "It's your fault we're late, I'm sick and tired of your dilly-dallying!" he may look askance if you reply: "You're speaking jackal language." He may not value your analysis. What you can do is silently observe that he is in his jackal and don your giraffe ears, so you can listen to what is bothering him. I will say more about giraffe ears in Chapter 5.

I have provided you with a basis on which to start making conscious choices about how you want to express yourself. Perhaps the following questions will be of help. Does one type of language appeal more to you than the other? With which language do you have the most experience? Would you be able or willing to miss one of the two languages?

An element that isn't specifically named in the model, but in my opinion, forms an essential part of it, is *thinking*. I also prefer to speak of the *ideas* of Nonviolent Communication rather than of the model. Language, whether spoken or unspoken, cannot exist without thinking. Without thought, our lives would be chaos. By thinking, we create frameworks and structure. Thinking is what makes us human. We can think about what has been, think about what could be in the future or bring our thoughts into the now between past and future.

So what about the thinking done by the giraffe and the jackal within? This is how I see it. The jackal has a smaller capacity for thought than the giraffe. When the jackal hears or sees something, he isolates himself from the outside world and in his old familiar way, uses his knowledge and his fantasy to think about what could happen. The door to his feelings, and so to his heart and his guts, is kept locked tight. Feelings might distract him. The thoughts he already has are reinforced and elaborated on. He develops an image of the world that no longer has much to do with reality. In this way, the jackal in each of us creates his own world, which he then compares with that of others. If we think our world is better than other people's, we try to convince them that we are right. If we think our world is worse, we tend to betray ourselves by competing with others and are unhappy if we don't succeed.

Krishnamurti, the Indian philosopher from the last century, writes the following about knowledge. He says we need knowledge for practical and technical matters. He read very few books himself. He wanted to understand the world and himself by observing them. According to him, knowledge stands in the way of radical inner change for the 'good'.

The giraffe thinks with his head, heart and guts. His senses remain open while he thinks, so depending on the ever-changing incoming sensory impressions, he can alter the direction of his thoughts. I don't know where the seat of thought actually is, if it is somewhere, or where it comes from. I have the idea that thoughts are given to us from the spiritual world and that we have the choice of whether to accept them or not. I am able to understand things better by using images, which is why I locate my thoughts in my head, heart and guts.

The thinking that goes on in my head orders things, under-stands, fills in details in the larger picture. My heart takes care of peace and selflessness. If I allow my heart into the equation, my feelings and my thoughts can influence each other. I stay in connection with what's happening in the moment and how I and others are responding to it inwardly. If my heart assists in my thinking, I get closer to my (or the?) truth. I can concentrate better, or stay in the now, and I am more creative, unhindered by the ballast of my knowledge.

My guts know what I need. I often literally feel it in my guts if something is demanding my attention. Just as I can feel butterflies in my stomach, I can sometimes feel a certain pressure or restlessness or squirming. I pay attention to the feeling and it helps me to get clear about what it is I need.

The giraffe sticks his neck out and has a broad outlook. The jackal directs all his attention towards his prey and views the world as it were, through a funnel. I would call jackal thinking exclusive thinking, and giraffe thinking, inclusive thinking.

I use these terms here for processes taking place in our inner world. They are also used when referring to our relationships with the external world. 'Inclusive thinking' has become the subject of much interest. It involves thinking from an awareness of oneness: we are all one, and everything we individually do and say has an influence on the whole. Books such as *The Field* by Lynne McTaggert and films such as *What the Bleep do we Know* go into this more extensively. 'Exclusive thinking' involves experiencing ourselves as separate from the rest, alone, just as everyone else is alone; each of us, a small island.

In these senses too, inclusive thinking fits the giraffe better and exclusive thinking, the jackal.

I am a friend of Aardewerkplaats Amiel, a place where people live and work on organic design and social plastics. We practice inclusive thinking there. We call it 'keeping each other in consciousness'. While we are each doing our own thing - working on a sculpture in a studio, cooking food for the group, teaching a group, fitting an electric socket, or painting at the top of a ladder - we keep our antennae out and remain conscious of the others' presence. We cultivate an encouraging, kindly attitude towards one another and towards what each of us is working on. I experience this as being very supportive and I feel safe and strong in it. Together, it's as if we create a dome of light in which our qualities can blossom.

As I practice this, I notice that my capacity for inclusive thought grows. When I'm walking along a busy shopping street, I can take the passers-by into my consciousness and accept them as they are. I do this sometimes when I'm in a traffic-jam or at the cinema. When I work with groups, I am doing it all the time. There was a time when this surprised me. How could I feel so much love for all these different people? Now I understand what I'm doing. I step into my giraffe and become one with him.

This union can be experienced in all sorts of situations. When we watch or listen to the news, we can feel our one-ness with the people involved in wars: leaders of government, soldiers, victims and those who protest against war. We can see them all as people just trying to live and survive, and we can empathize with their feelings and needs. During political debates, we can look at the factors motivating each politician and thus understand them better (which is a different thing from agreeing with them). We may need a pair of extra large giraffe ears to accomplish this, especially if we are used to listening with jackal ears.

We can apply this social art to the world of insurance too. Let us consider health insurance. We pay our annual contribution. If we have had a healthy year for a change and visited the doctor hardly or not at all, we could see paying our contribution as a waste of money: nothing for something.

We can look at it in another way. We all pay our contributions and in return, we have the security of knowing that we will not be confronted with exorbitant bills. And we pay our contributions not only for our own security but also so that others can enjoy this security too. So collectively, we carry everyone's health-costs. Since I realized this, I am perfectly happy making as little use of my insurance as I do. I am also happy to make a contribution to other people's care and security.

The giraffe is a land-mammal with a very large heart. Its heart has to be powerful enough to pump the blood all the way up through that long neck to the brains. The heart stands for love, for generously allowing ourselves to receive and for giving generously from our hearts. We are all familiar with the expression: 'He (or she) has a big heart'. What we mean by this is that the person can imagine himself (or herself) in the other's shoes and forgive, as a mother does this for her child as he travels through the ups and downs of life.

It has been proved that we have more energy, deal more adequately with life and are more creative if our hearts and our brains are connected and in balance with each other (see The Inside Story and other books, published by the HeartMath Institute).

The jackal has long been a symbol that fits snugly with our human ideas of death and evil spirits. The Egyptian god Anubis was depicted with the head of a jackal. It was said of Anubis that he escorted the dead to the gods for their final judgment. This association may have arisen from the jackal's habit of hunting at night or from his haunting howl, drifting to our ears across dark lands.

What intrigues me is that although Anubis delivered the dead to their last judgment, he did not pass judgment himself. He acted as a guide. I think the function of the jackal within is similar. With his uncensored language and bold actions, he leads us towards that divine spark within us and expects a wise, loving response to it.

3 Can't we ditch the jackal and just be giraffes?

During my early acquaintance with the jackal and the giraffe, I thought the idea was to do my utmost to become a giraffe. I thought it would be wonderful if, from now on, I were to be understanding of everyone and everything. All I had to do was stick to observations and turn my attention to feelings and needs. And stop making demands, of course.

I found however that it wasn't that easy to act upon this resolution. I'm a brilliant 'interpreter' for instance: I tend to think I know what someone else is thinking or intends to say. This struck me as a good place to make a start and I took a decision. From now on, I was going to stick to the facts, not fill things in any more, which only leads to misunderstandings, as in the following example.

I do *qi gong*, a movement discipline from China, and a dear friend of mine once told me that *qi gong* is bad for the health. He thought it would be better if I stopped. Some time later, he asked how it was going with my *qi gong*. I immediately went on the defensive: he obviously wanted to know if I had stopped yet and if not, if I had already become ill. At least, that's what I thought he wanted to know. It didn't occur to me that he might be asking out of interest. My friend was astonished at my fierce reaction. He had long ago accepted that *qi gong* was apparently my 'thing' and had become curious.

When, as in this example, I still used to make the occasional interpretation, I used to take myself to task about it. I was impatient at myself: I knew how nonviolent communication was done now, so I should just get on with it.

Fortunately, I arrived at the insight that by rigorously ceasing to make interpretations, I was betraying a part of myself. I was denying myself the pleasure I had experienced when I concocted entire stories about the people I observed. Like at a camp-site, when I saw two young couples talking to each other, while their children, both aged about two, played near by. I imagined that they had just met each other and were talking about their children. I was sure they all four had busy jobs and were now enjoying just relaxing and chatting.

When I allow myself to fantasize in this way, I am also training my powers of observation. As I watch and muse, I wonder where I get the idea that they all four work or that they're just enjoying relaxing. I don't want to know if it's true. It's a game. At such times, I'm enjoying my jackal, who thinks he knows exactly how things work.

I am gradually learning to call in my giraffe as well, as soon as I notice that I'm losing connection with myself or someone else or that an argument is threatening - as in the *qi gong* example. When I went on the defensive on that occasion, my friend became angry. I put on my giraffe ears and said: "Are you angry because you think I'm on the defensive?" This gave him the space to tell me that he felt hurt. He felt sad at the idea of me thinking all this time that he disapproved of me practicing *qi gong*. He wanted recognition for the fact that he respected my choices and was genuinely interested in what I did. Thanks to my giraffe, our connection was restored and the confrontation did not degenerate into a hail of poisoned arrows.

I didn't give my jackal the opportunity of growing into a full-blown adult jackal. While he was still a baby jackal, had only just taken an interest and only just begun to splutter his protest, my giraffe had already bent his head down close to him. My giraffe gave him some attention, provided for his needs and he was able to go back to sleep again.

If we do this, the jackal is able to fulfill the function I think he is supposed to fulfill. He sends out alarm-signals when needs are unfulfilled and the giraffe picks them up and takes appropriate action.

It sounds so simple. The jackal announces himself, the giraffe talks to him and harmony is restored. Before the giraffe is able to do this reliably however, he needs some practice.

The giraffe too, starts out as a baby. At birth, he radiates only Love. Ever seen a baby wake up in the middle of the night and send out signals to its parents in the vein of: "Oi, lazybones, get up! Can't you hear I'm hungry? Your duty is to take care of me whether you like it or not"? No, babies just make requests. By crying, they let us know they are hungry. A baby will still be happy to see his parents even if they come to him only after an hour. No accusations, just love.

As, later in life and now consciously, we get in touch with our giraffes, we may be pretty clumsy with them to begin with. Giraffes will want to respond to their surroundings with understanding but are as yet unable to always find the appropriate words. They start out falteringly and to a raging jackal, may only manage: "Er, are you feeling irritated and do you, er, need understanding?"

But giraffes grow up and at a certain point, reach puberty. They understand that it's okay to stand up for themselves and do so with vitality. I meet some 'teenage' giraffes like this in the course of my work. Imagine fifteen people sitting in a circle. One person interrupts the conversation with the words: "I'm not feeling connected. I need connection." And then looks around with an expectant air as if to say: "Make the connection happen, now." Or he responds to a remark someone makes with: "What need makes you say that?"

And this 'teenager' doesn't want to listen to anything else until a satisfactory answer has been given.

What he fails to realize is that while he has gone into his own inner process by making contact with his own feelings and needs, he has as yet made no contact with the feelings and needs of others. He doesn't realize that he can restore his connection with the group by opening himself up to what is alive in the group. And if that doesn't work, by waiting for a suitable moment to speak.

A 'teenage' giraffe who, out of a conviction that his feelings have never counted, has always kept his feelings to himself, can at this stage of development, be quite effluvious about his irritation or his sadness, whether others are interested or not.

I also know some 'teenage' jackals. You might think a baby jackal, listened to directly with giraffe ears, would be satisfied with a quick grumble. In practice, I have noticed that when a jackal is given space, he sometimes has the tendency to let all his inhibitions go and spit venom. Bottled up judgments and irritations emerge, unrelated to the moment. My giraffe responds to this with a smile and quietly continues to translate the poison into feelings and needs. It's easy to see when I've done enough. There's a big sigh or the person's body relaxes: in other words, his or her giraffe takes over and restores the connection with what's alive at that moment.

To return to the resolution with which I started this chapter (to be understanding of everyone at all times): what I also tried to do initially was to stop making judgments and every time I caught myself doing it, I'd beat myself up about it. I was actually judging myself, being a jackal to myself. I was unaware of this and started feeling increasingly weighed down and discouraged.

I am not the only one to have fallen into this trap. I was once giving a workshop lasting six evenings. On the second evening, a young woman said: "I manage to be a giraffe quite well at work this week. But when I come home in the evening, I'm exhausted. I don't understand it".

What was exhausting her? Suppressing her inner jackal. As soon as her jackal wanted to speak, she would gag him. She would hide him under her chair, sit on him. She would do her very best to ignore him, to pretend he didn't exist, as I did in the story at the beginning of this book. Just think how we feel when we're ignored, when no-one wants to listen to us. We feel frustrated, we fight for attention. We kick up a fuss or set our sights on revenge. It takes other people more and more effort to ignore us, so it can get pretty exhausting.

When we exhaust ourselves trying to ignore our own jackals, we will very probably blame other people or the circumstances. Because that's what jackals do.

So we can see that any attempt to ditch the jackal actually leads to the opposite. The jackal just grows bigger and fiercer. And more and more jackals come to join him. Each jackal provokes another jackal which then tries to see off his predecessor. Until there's an entire pack. How can we prevent these jackals from ruling our thoughts and actions, from ranting and raving to such a degree that our giraffes barely get a look-in, if any at all? We can achieve this by taking each and every jackal seriously, by listening to what's beneath or behind his blame and judgments. Jackals want to let us know when a need is not being met but they are not known for their subtlety and do this in a language which is, alas, all too familiar in this day and age. If we receive these signals and seek out the unfulfilled needs, our jackals will be contented and go back to sleep. In this way, they remain small and harmless.

This principle applies both to the jackals battling within us and to the jackals out there in the big bad world. Peace activists employ this same empathy to the feelings and needs of both war-mongers and terrorists, and to their victims, hungry for revenge. The larger the herds of giraffes we send out to our theatres of war, the earlier peace will come into focus. Everyone who empathizes with those leading violent lives provides an opportunity of healing the underlying pain, making space in these people for their giraffes to stand tall.

What I am saying is that the jackal has a function. He draws our attention to our unfulfilled needs. He shouts for attention, and the more we ignore him, the louder he will shout.

It is not always easy to translate his blunt remarks. We may be forgiven for not realizing that: "Get the hell out of here!" may mean "I need some rest". It demands a combination of clarity of awareness and unending mildness and patience.

I do not recommend trying to ban the jackal to the underworld. He'll bide his time there in the darkness, brooding upon further violence. If we give him space – see him, hear him – we'll find he loves it. Once he has received sufficient attention, he will quietly retreat and go to sleep. Only when there are no giraffes around does a jackal get really dangerous.

I advise people to visit a 'jackal café' from time to time. This is a term thought up by Bridget Belgrave and Gina Lawrie, two Nonviolent Communication trainers from England. The jackal café is where your jackals can meet each other and unabashedly blow off steam. Just think of the conversations you might overhear in an ordinary café or a pub.

"I went to the dentist's today. They're all the same. You can never get a word in edgeways yourself. It's just: 'mouth open and shut up'. As it were." "I know just what you mean. My dentist replaced three fillings, nothing wrong with any of them. Without so much as a by-your-leave. But he didn't forget the bill. Outrageous." "They're extortionists!" "If he shows his face in this pub, I'll knock his teeth out for him. Give me another beer."

On occasion, I have tried to break into a conversation like this, placing my giraffe up on the bar in my imagination. "Are you angry because you'd like your dentist to discuss things with you before he does anything?" The success of attempts such as this depends to a degree on the skills of the giraffe and to a degree on the number of beers already consumed.

In Nonviolent Communication, the jackal café is a place we can go to allow our jackals off the leash for a little. We look for a place removed from those who have triggered our anger: alone in our own rooms, in the company of a friend or on a course.

In this café, our jackals are allowed to vent their anger freely. Jackals do this in a different way from giraffes. Giraffes feel the anger in their bodies and take responsibility for it themselves. They may say: "I'm angry because I don't want to wait." Jackals give other people the blame: "I'm angry because YOU are late." We may seek the cause of our anger outside ourselves, but it is always inside us.

In the jackal café, self-examination can wait. The jackal is given some extra space by allowing him to split off into separate jackals and by allowing each one to have his say. One may be blaming, another judging, yet another may pontificate about how things ought to be or how someone should be punished. The victim jackal claims helplessness. And the various jackals can also react to one another. One jackal may for instance say: "Who's left the washing up again?" and another may say: "That idiot George, of course."

It's important not to try to look at underlying needs too soon. If we do this before giving a jackal a true hearing and taking him seriously, he'll get the idea that he's not welcome, that it's wrong to be angry like this. The more of our lives we have spent suppressing our anger, the more room our jackals will need now. Let them stamp their feet, beat on cushions. Not that this will solve anything in itself. If we were to leave it at that, our anger would just grow and become more obstinate. But just giving the anger some air, both verbally and physically, can help some of the anger to disappear.

To actually transform the judging and blaming, the giraffe's presence is of essential importance. A method I find very liberating is to first feel the anger, then give one jackal a chance to speak and then return to feeling the anger. I then give the next jackal to appear some airtime and go back to the anger again and so on until I'm done and feeling calm. Only then do I start looking for the underlying needs.

Anger isn't the only cause of jackal behavior. It can be fear, guilt or shame too. We rage then not at somebody else, but at ourselves. We're afraid we'll catch hell because we've done something wrong. We're ashamed of something and blame ourselves for what's gone wrong. In this case, the judging and blaming is aimed at ourselves.

The jackal's presence is not always a signal of unfulfilled needs. We are already fulfilling a need just by being a jackal. In fact, everything we do is to fulfill a need, or we wouldn't do it. So what are the advantages of being a jackal? If we use our jackal to manipulate, he gives us power. I don't see power as a basic need, so what might be behind it? If I have power, I feel safe. There's a basic need: safety. The people over whom I have power do what I tell them, so my need to be heard is met. I have control over the situation and that gives me order and clarity.

Reading this, you may be thinking that being a jackal isn't all that bad. Alas, what we have here is only temporary need-fulfillment. In the long run, if we have power, we will notice that our need for safety goes unmet, as we are likely to be perpetually afraid of others trying to undermine it by secretively doing what we have forbidden. And while we may be listened to, it will only be when we are acting from our office of power or if we raise our voice. Not if we have a problem or feel insecure. People will avoid us then and we will become lonely. On top of this, while we are exerting power, our need to make a contribution to others' happiness won't be fulfilled. And that is a universal human need too.

During certain periods of our lives or in certain circumstances, we are jackals most of the time, and at other times, we are predominantly giraffes. I am convinced that we all have both the jackal and the giraffe in us. A person can be as hard as nails and bitter with it, but they can still be moved by the sight of a young puppy or genuinely worried for the health of a child. A person can be very patient and loving at work and with friends and acquaintances, and still blow up at his wife when he comes home exhausted.

By the way, if we speak of ourselves as giraffes and thereby imply that we are better than others, we give ourselves away immediately. The idea that I am better than another is already a jackal thought.

We just need to be happy with our jackals. Make friends with them. See them as bringers of gifts. But we do need to unpack these gifts to find out what feelings and needs are inside.

We need to be happy with other people's jackals too; our partner's, for instance. Try to unpack one of these gifts today. Suppose the note on the gift-wrapping says: "I've completely had it with you. You always have to get your own way." If we unpack this what do we find? We'll find out what the person is trying to say: "When I heard you say: "we're doing it this way and that's final", I felt powerless. I need to be heard. Would you listen to what I would like?" Watch what happens if we respond to the contents rather than to the note on the wrapping paper.

The giraffe has a strong, tough tongue, with the texture of something akin to rubber or plastic. This means that he can chew on thorns without coming to harm. Translated into human terms, this means that when we're 'in our giraffe' we're able to 'chew up' the aggressive words of the jackal and turn them into harmless food without damaging ourselves. Think of the expression: 'I find what you're saying hard to digest'. Perhaps the messages we hear will become more digestible if we get ourselves fitted out with giraffe tongues.

Giraffe tongues are also long, so they can easily fold themselves around the long thorns of the acacia tree. They don't run away from the jackal's vitriol. They surround it with love.

In the word 'jackal' we find the word 'jack'. The different sources I consulted did not agree on the etymological link between 'jackal' and 'jack', but I enjoy playing with associations.

The English language is full of 'jacks', often with a wicked or negative connotation. To mention a few, a 'Jack-a-dandy' stands for a 'silly person', a 'Jack-in-office' is a self-important civil servant and a 'Jack-in-the-box' is a little devil. The Dutch verb 'jakhalzen' (=to jackal) is used in the East Friesian dialect for 'to long for something strongly'. I find recognition in these expressions for the idea that a jackal is a villainous, stupid or silly person who longs for the fulfillment of his needs for autonomy, appreciation, rest and space or any other need.

In jackal society the social unit is that of a monogamous pair which defends its territory from other pairs. These territories are defended by vigorously chasing intruding rivals away and marking landmarks around the territory with urine and feces.

4 Being a giraffe versus acting like a giraffe

If we want to be jackals, we should be jackals and if we want to be giraffes, we should be giraffes. We shouldn't try to suppress the jackal. In the previous chapter, we have seen what can happen if we do. We get tired, and possibly even depressed or ill. A part of us gets left out and dies off. We are actually only half alive. If we don't listen to the jackal, if we pretend he doesn't exist, we can *play* the giraffe, but it will not help us to be in genuine contact with other people. The important question is whether we can be 'congruent': whether we can really, genuinely, from the inside as well as on the outside *be* giraffes.

If 'jackaling' has become a sort of automatism, we may well genuinely intend to be a giraffe but, before we know it and without wanting to, we revert to our jackal form. Suppose we want to listen to someone attentively. They say something about the importance of sharing tasks equally, but we think it's more important to do what we do with pleasure than to share things equally. We want to keep our opinion out of the conversation, but we start asking questions like: "What's so important about sharing equally? It's just as important that everyone enjoys his work." And before we know it, we're in the dogmatic world of the jackal. Watchfulness is required here.

As soon as we find ourselves listening to our own judgments, we no longer really have room to listen to somebody else. If we then have a good old 'jackal' as we did in the jackal café of the last chapter, it may help us to blow off some steam. I don't mean that we should do this at the person whose words or actions triggered our frustration, sadness or disappointment. No, I mean we should take the time to sit down somewhere quietly and listen to our jackal. Or jackals. Allow them to file past and give each one his turn to speak: the blamer, the know-all, the victim, the prescriber of norms, the avenger.

If this doesn't work because we're just not calm enough, we can seek some kind of physical outlet for our emotions. We can go and chop wood, scrub the kitchen floor or go for a run. Some therapists encourage people to take their emotions out on a cushion or bash an old telephone book with a piece of garden hose. As a child, I learned to suppress my anger.

When I was about 47, I went through a period of feeling safe enough to work my old anger out of my body. I would look for excuses. René, my partner, had for instance made a 'vicious remark'. First, I'd begin to scream at him and when he fled the room, I'd go even further. I'd thump the wall with my fists. Or I'd get a pan-lid out of the cupboard and bash it on the ground again and again as hard as I could. The racket this made, in combination with exerting my full force, was very liberating.

Another time, it was my tears I let loose. René and I had known each other for six months. We were spending a few days in a hotel in Germany. We were eating dinner after a harmonious day in the country together. At a certain point, he said something about a painting. I was moved and I was trying to tell him so. He was so wrapped up in his own thoughts that he didn't focus on my feelings, but went on with his blah-blah-blah. And suddenly, all the times I had not been heard or taken seriously rose to the surface. I threw down my serviette and ran to our room, where I let my panic and sorrow take over completely. I was trembling and shaking and crying. René had followed me upstairs and stayed with me. When I had finished shaking and crying, he was all ears.

I don't think giving space to emotions in itself greatly contributes to transforming our jackals. As long as we're convinced that someone else is the cause of our emotions and that it's up to them to change the world so we can be happy, any ranting and raving will just feed the jackal. We will just become more dogmatic in our judgments.

So we need to get the giraffe involved. He can throw his light on our distress and seek out our feelings and needs. We may not be able to do this immediately if we have been hurt deeply. We give someone else the blame for the pain and think they should see to it that we come out of it as soon as possible. I notice that I open my door to let in the giraffe with increasing speed, because I want to. I have decided to take responsibility for my own process and I need my giraffe to be able to do that. In situations such as those I have described above, I would have remained in my jackal if, in my anger and misery, I had continued to blame the other person. As soon as my anger and misery became impersonal, in the sense of not being directed at someone, I was a giraffe, in contact with her feelings.

If our jackal is so lively that we are momentarily unable to find our giraffe, we could ask someone else to function as a giraffe and translate for us, because we need an interpreter for our jackal language. Suppose the boss always gets us to do his dirty work and as far as we're concerned, he can get lost. If we first get this off our chest by talking to a friend or neighbor, we may discover that we wouldn't mind doing the occasional dirty job if the boss were just to ASK instead of ordering us around and if he'd occasionally show his appreciation. Only then are we ready to speak to the 'culprit'. The jackal can climb back into his basket and the giraffe can take over.

Whether we are able to perform the transformation from jackal to giraffe ourselves, or whether we get help from others, the transformation is a prerequisite for *being* a real giraffe.

In the following example, we will see what happens if we try to act the giraffe while not *being* it. How a jackal in giraffe's clothing tries to apply the Nonviolent Communication model to get his own way.

Connie, a participant in one of my workshops has been trying for more than a year to get rid of her internet provider
because, due to a fault of theirs, she has been unable to make
use of their services. She was threatened with the bailiffs
because she hadn't paid her bills. She was desperate and
said that in spite of everything, she had always been polite
and friendly in all her letters and during all her telephone
calls. She thought that if she kept pleasantly repeating that
the company had made a mistake, they would eventually
see she was right. She told her story, under the impression
that she was being a real giraffe, and didn't understand why
the problem had not been solved.

As I worked with her, we discovered that she was full of
judgments about how she had been treated and that she'd
really like to tell the director just what she thought of him.
She didn't do this because she was afraid that she would lose
the battle entirely if she did. At a certain point, someone
from the group said: "If I were the director, I'd say I was in
a meeting next time you rang. I'd feel extremely uncomfortable listening to someone being polite and friendly while
I could tell she didn't mean a word of it, even down the
phone-line. I'd rather you screamed at me. At least I'd know
where I stood with you".

Connie had ignored her jackal and gone through the motions of being a giraffe. Now, she was giving her jackal some
room for air and we gave her some empathy. We listened
to her story about these 'idiotic' people without telling her
she was right or trying to lessen the impact. We echoed
how miserable it was for her to have spent so much time
on this problem without arriving at a satisfactory solution.
We heard her worry. Just imagine if she had to pay this bill!
She didn't have much money in the first place.

Afterwards, she felt relieved and practiced how she could be a proper giraffe next time she spoke to them. She would express her frustration and her desperation, she would be angry, but without judging. She might for instance say: "I'm very angry because I haven't had internet for a year now and have also spent vast amounts of time trying to solve this misunderstanding about the service delivery. I am sick and tired of it and perhaps you are too. Would you please look at this with me and see if we can find a solution and close this drama once and for all?" The words 'and perhaps you are too' now come from the heart. She wants peace for herself, but also for the people at the internet company.

This inner work takes time. It can be a difficult battle, but it can be playful too. Once I had made a mistake and charged a workshop participant less than I wanted to receive. I sent him an e-mail to explain this and asked if he would be prepared to pay the full amount. His reply was: "Just a moment, I'm thinking about it." Three days later, he wrote back. He had initially felt angry and irritated. If he had reacted immediately, his jackal would have spoken: "Are you crazy? What's agreed is agreed. I knew what you were charging, but I was quite happy to pay less. And I think it's pretty unprofessional of you to ask for more money now. You shouldn't advertise your mistakes and you should take responsibility for their consequences."

He realized that he was a bit tired of this sort of response. In my workshop, he had learned alternatives and he decided first to feel his anger, then to look for his underlying needs and finally, to send me a giraffe e-mail. He discovered that paying a lower price had answered his needs for ease and safety. He didn't have that much money, so my mistake suited him fine. He also remembered that he had decided to do the workshop for my originally intended price. And he had enjoyed the workshop and felt a connection with me.

So his feeling of ease (through listening to his conscience) and respect for both himself and for me would be met by paying the full amount. He chose to meet these needs and told me the money was on its way.

He could of course, have expressed his anger to his friends by telling them how stupid and unreliable I was, while out of a desire to be civil, going through the motions of being a giraffe and paying me the missing amount. In this way, he would have strengthened his conviction that 'trainers are untrustworthy' and broken the connection with me.

The Belgian writer Thomas D'Ansembourg wrote a book entitled 'Being Genuine: Stop Being Nice, Start Being Real'. The last part emphasizes that we need to 'Be Real' whatever happens. So be nice if we really feel the niceness we're communicating. And be angry and irritated if that's the way we feel. Whether we actually show, let alone speak, of our anger and irritation will depend. It's a question of assessing the situation, a perfect job for our intuition.

This *being* real is something I don't always find easy. I was brought up to be a good little girl and that little girl is afraid of being punished. Sometimes, she climbs up onto the giraffe's neck and then she appears friendly and magnanimous. She can pretend she's a giraffe, but she's hanging onto the outside of the giraffe's neck, she doesn't climb inside it.

I find it very difficult to stay 'real' when someone talks in generalizations. "You can't trust anyone these days." My hackles or my jackal whiskers rise immediately. Where is the world going to if we place ourselves in a glass cage and blame the rest of the world for everything and more. And anyway, how am I supposed to respond? I want to know who we're talking about and what he did to damage this person's trust. When I'm in touch with the well-behaved little girl in me, I continue to smile politely and make an attempt to connect with the other person: "Would you like to be able to trust more people?" Inwardly, I'm shifting uneasily in my seat and I'm already looking forward to telling a friend about what an idiot I met this time.

I was at a birthday party recently. During a conversation about the coming elections, I met a man who responded in a way I'd like to learn from. Each time someone started generalizing more than was to his taste, he said something like: "It's getting too abstract for me. Could you give me an example?" His words, his attitude and the tone in which he spoke, demonstrated his genuine interest in what had moved the person to arrive at these generalizations. I recognized his interest. I have that too. Although not always. I realize that I'm not always interested and not in everyone. I'm going to make a choice in future. I'll either be a jackal, silently judging the chatterer and moving on to another subject, or I'll choose to deepen my contact with the person because I want to. Then I will no longer be being 'good' but genuinely interested.

Am I not forgetting one possibility? We've had the jackal I keep to myself (being real doesn't mean spewing jackal language all over other people just because we feel like it). We've also had the giraffe with genuine interest for what's alive in other people.

Oh yes, I know. I nearly forgot about being a giraffe to myself: examining my feelings and needs and standing up for them, speaking out. I was still being nicer and less real than I had sworn I would be. Here it comes then, better late than never: "When I hear you say "You can't trust anyone these days", I feel irritated because I don't really know what you mean, then my connection with you disappears and I want to be connected. Who is 'anyone' and which days are 'these days'? Would you give me an example of someone you don't trust any more and tell me what led to this?"

Sometimes there isn't a single giraffe to be found, wherever I look. I had just dealt pleasantly with two telephone conversations while I was feeling anything but pleasant inside. My e-mail program had snarled up on me and I could see how badly my house needed cleaning. Then René came home at seven o'clock when I was due to give a lecture at eight and he had promised to cook. Waddaya mean, giraffe? My jackal started to rage, before the front door had even closed: "You're unbelievably late. You know I've got to leave at half past seven. I haven't eaten a thing, because you said you'd cook. You're useless. You never do what you say." René, a sculptor, had just had a bad day. A piece of a sculpture had broken off and the wax of another had melted because it was too close to the heater. He just gave as good as he got. He just jackaled right back at me.

Rosenberg's advice, in a situation like this is: 'to enjoy the jackal show'. A solid relationship can take it. When both partners have blown off steam, they'll notice that the giraffe will present himself and do what is necessary to restore the peace. René and I usually separate for a few minutes. Once the storm has abated in one of us, he or she looks carefully to see if the other's jackal has had as much attention as he wants. Then we repair our connection with a hug or a joke. In the above case, René quickly made me a cheese omelet, and while I ate it, I listened to the tale of everything that had gone wrong with his day.

Looking at the jackal in ourselves and in those around us with mildness and humor is essential to the success of the giraffe-jackal concept. The jackal no longer has to pretend he's a giraffe and the giraffe can be a true giraffe. Of course, no-one will object if we strive to be giraffes more and more of the time. I just recommend that we do it only if we are enjoying it. And if we're not enjoying it, we must take care of ourselves for just as long as it takes until we can really enjoy being giraffes again from our hearts.

But it takes time to regain that enjoyment. So what do we do now, in the present, if we don't want to jackal at our conversation partner? We could say out loud what's going on inside us: "I notice I'm making some judgments and I don't want to do that." This will help us to release our grip on the judgments and the other person will know what's going on, so he can stay in connection. It may be that this is not enough, that more time is needed. We can then take a 'time out'. We don't just walk away, but we say something to the other person like: "If I continue now, I'm going to say things I'll regret. I'm going to withdraw." In this way, the connection remains intact, even if we leave the room. The connection is broken if we storm out of the room without a word and slam the door behind us.

Sometimes, I can take the time to examine my judgments and give them a place in my heart, while remaining where I am, but falling silent. I listen both to what the other is saying and to what is going on inside me. I get in touch with my feelings and my needs. This works if my conversation partner and I are doing something together: driving, making a sandwich in the kitchen, or working in the garden. If the other person notices, starts to feel uncomfortable, and says something like: "Why have you stopped talking?" I will explain what I'm doing. This is a calm, nourishing silence: very different from the laden silences we can get if we just suddenly stop talking while thinking that the other person should sort it out for themselves, because we then step out of connection.

I get more and more fun out of translating my judgments and pausing to look at how things affect me. I'll line up some jackal and giraffe responses so we can compare:

"What a lousy road!" becomes "This road is so bad, I daren't drive faster than 20mph and I really want to get home soon."

"Just listen to that father ranting on, it's awful!" becomes "When I see that man speaking to his children like that, I feel miserable because I really value qualities like patience and respect."

"Are those people talking about ruddy football again?!" becomes "I wish they'd be quiet because I'm sitting here in the same bus trying to read a book."

By making this shift, I'm no longer occupied with everything I think should change in the world (but about which I am either unable or unwilling to do anything). I don't want to go and re-level that road or write a letter about it to the council. I don't want to re-educate the father. I don't want to spoil the football fans' fun. I am aware of the effect my surroundings have on me and if necessary, I empathize with myself. I no longer try to force other people to change or convince them of my values by being 'friendly' or a so-called 'giraffe'. I can leave the responsibility where it belongs, which gives me a light, free feeling. I feel free to live with my own nature and my own values.

According to Rosenberg, we are all natural giraffes. Just look at children. They watch keenly, free from judgment. They follow their hearts. They show their feelings openly and if they are having a good time themselves, they enjoy giving others a good time. I know, children can also be selfish, and shout, hit and bite if they don't get their way. At moments like these, their desire to contribute to the happiness of others is taking a rest, while other needs require attention.

My experience with young children is that if someone hears their unfulfilled needs, children return to happiness and love very easily. Because it is their nature.

As his nature so closely resembles our own nature, the giraffe within can easily put us in touch with our intuition, an inner knowledge that we cannot logically explain. We can, for instance, sometimes physically feel in our bodies, in our guts, that we should stay out of someone's way.

I was once on holiday in Greece and went to a barbecue. I was having a good time with everyone, but there was one man of whom I knew, the moment I saw him, that I would be wise to avoid. He seemed friendly and was part of the crowd enjoying the party. The following morning, I heard that, on his way to the tents, he had tried to rape a woman he had talked to and danced with at the party.

In order to gain more certainty about the truth and value of my intuition, I have trained myself to use my observation to complement it. In the case above, my intuition had warned me about the man at the barbecue. I started to observe him to find out if my first impression was correct. I then noticed things that other people perhaps did not notice. For instance, he reached for a basket of French bread right in front of someone else's nose, just when this person was about to put something into his mouth, which to my mind, hinted at a not fully developed ability to put himself in someone else's shoes.

Between his large, flexible ears standing bolt upright on his head, the giraffe has two short horns and between these a third horn, which never fully develops. It's a bump under the skin at the exact location of the third eye. According to ancient traditions, we have a connection at that point with the Higher, the spiritual world.

For me, the two outer horns stand for intuition, antennae with which to observe what remains hidden to the senses. This leads to an inner knowledge. I recommend that we take the information we receive through our 'horns' seriously, but without trusting it blindly. There's a fine line between interpretation and intuition. I've developed the habit of putting on my little horns as much of the time as possible, so observation and intuition can complement each other perfectly.

In North American folk tales, the jackal takes on roughly the same role as the fox in the Reynard the Fox stories. The African jackal gets his come-uppance even more frequently than his European counterpart.

I once read a story from Northern Algeria, in which a stork drops a jackal from a great height into a pond, from which he crawls, shaking with cold. I thought this 'birth trauma' might well trigger distrust in the jackal and a yearning to control his own life whatever the cost. And sure enough, a little further along in the story, I read of 'the jackal of a hundred wiles'.

5 Listening with giraffe or jackal ears

We use jackal language without thinking. We've been practicing it for generations (or for many lives, if we believe in reincarnation) so it has now become second nature. If we want to learn to speak giraffe language, we need to root out this second nature to re-reveal our ever-present underlying 'first nature'. Translating from jackal language into giraffe language has been mentioned earlier. In order to translate, we need a special listening skill. We hear and listen with our ears. But how we do both depends on the kind of ears we wear.

Within the framework of this book, it may appear logical to assume that we have two different sorts of ears: giraffe ears and jackal ears. This is true, but we can also put these ears on our heads in two different ways. With the opening facing outwards, listening to the other or others, or with the ears facing inwards, listening to ourselves. So I speak of the four ways we can listen or the 'four pairs of ears'.

When we are wearing our jackal ears facing outwards, we think the other person is trying to manipulate or undermine us. We hear blame and accusation. With our jackal ears facing inwards, we hear a voice telling us the other person is right: we *are* bad or stupid. Or the voice tells us we're lax, impatient or lazy. Listening to ourselves with our jackal ears turned inwards leads to guilt, shame and depression. All our energy drains away and we become insecure and apathetic. These two positions of our jackal ears can alternate at lightning speed. Anger – guilt, shame and depression – anger – guilt, shame and…

With our giraffe ears facing inwards, we hear what's going on inside us or what effect a remark from outside has had on us. What are we feeling? What are our needs? We take the time to listen to ourselves and give ourselves empathy. With the giraffe ears turned outwards, we no longer hear blame or accusation. We hear the feelings and needs of the person speaking to us. Whether the person is actually accusing us of something or whether we are used to interpreting it as such, we no longer hear it as blame.

Suppose a friend says to me: "I feel very insecure around you, because you always know everything so much better."

Let's have a look at what I hear through the four different sets of ears.

- The *jackal ears facing outwards* hear an attack from my friend: "It's your fault I feel so insecure. You should hold back a bit more." My jackal then reacts with: "Nice try, putting the blame for your insecurity on me, but you're not getting away with it."

- The *jackal ears facing inwards* hear my reaction to her words: "You see, she's right. I always have to let the whole world know that I know better." If I openly admit to this,

I draw the attention towards myself. It's suddenly about me and not about my friend. I completely pass over what it's like for her to experience the insecurity she's talking about. Or I go on the defensive and we arrive at a 'yes it is – no it isn't' deadlock: "You're exaggerating. Of course I don't always know everything. Whatever makes you say that?"

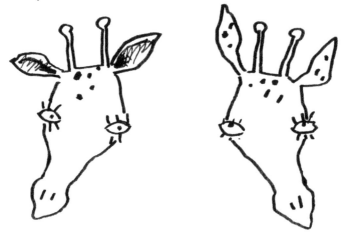

-   The *giraffe ears facing inwards* hear the effect the remark has had on me. "Ouch, she's touching a sensitive area. I know I can appear self-confident, especially when I'm feeling insecure. I wish I dared to show her my vulnerability more and dared to tell her how I'm really feeling sometimes." I can say this aloud and make a connection with her at the heart level. I can also keep it to myself for a bit and first deal with what she's saying. She may be able to give more attention to what is taking place in me in response to her remark if I first give some attention to her words.

-   The *giraffe ears facing outwards* hear what my friend meant to say: "I feel insecure when you say: "It just is that way.'" If I take the words 'always' and 'everything' out of what she said, the accusing tone disappears, and I can listen calmly to what she is saying. I might ask her what's lacking in our contact when I say something like that (what need remains unfulfilled) and what she would prefer.

These four steps can be used in the above order. They can also be used independently of each other, depending on what seems useful.

In dangerous situations, when there is a threat of physical violence for instance, I would recommend reaching immediately for the *giraffe ears facing outwards*. If someone's pain and frustration has reached such a pitch that he is about to explode, he can only be helped by a wave of empathy.

Whatever the situation, if our jackal ears perk up, we need to decide what we want. Do we have the time and inclination to fetch a pair of giraffe ears or will we just leave things as they are?

During the workshops and individual coaching sessions I give, I frequently meet people who skip the third step: the *giraffe ears facing inwards*. Sounds familiar? They judge other people and then judge themselves for being such a hard judge, or they just judge themselves for everything anyway, and then quickly pass on to the *giraffe ears facing outwards*. They notice that it's difficult, giving empathy, but don't realize why. The conversation is completed in a friendly manner. The other person goes on his way satisfied, and they feel tired and discontented because they have inflicted violence upon themselves.

In situations like this, I have a wealth of arguments with which to lead myself up the garden path. These may also sound familiar. I tell myself that I'm happy when others are happy. "I can handle a bit of give-and-take and actually, it wasn't that important." "She meant well and I shouldn't take things too personally." "I can take a knock." These are all ways of saying that I'm not worth taking seriously.

I now know that I can't really be available to others if I haven't taken care of myself, because if I don't, part of me is still confused, angry or miserable. I'm not empty; I don't have the space to let other people in.

It is possible to learn to take the time and space to listen to ourselves with giraffe ears. What exactly just happened? Why am I reacting like this? What feelings are being stimulated? What needs are not being met? We take the time to look at this, to feel what we feel and empathize with ourselves. There's no rush to solve anything. This is about taking ourselves seriously and mourning what is lacking. It's useful to listen to ourselves like this and not be dependent on someone else's listening ear.

We discover that listening to other people gives us pleasure and energy when we have first listened to ourselves. In this way, we are connected with ourselves as well as with the other person. By skipping the *giraffe ears facing inwards* step, we close off to our inner world and we don't really listen from our hearts to what's going on in the other person. The result is that we feel lonely.

When we have had some experience with this third step, and have gained some proficiency, we may need no more than a few seconds. We turn our giraffe ears inwards and 'see' a mixture of feelings and unmet needs. We embrace them, accepting ourselves the way we are and we're ready: ready to turn our ears outwards and give our full attention to the other person. We may need more time, either there in the moment or later, on our bikes home or writing in our diaries.

If this all sounds a bit theoretical and you need to see and experience it first hand to understand it, here are a few suggestions for practical exercises.

- With your hands make the shape of a pair of ears. Experiment until you have discovered what shape of ears will fit your giraffe and what shape will fit your jackal. Hold these 'ears' above your head, facing either inwards or outwards. See how it feels. Think of things you might say with each ear 'gesture', either to yourself or to someone else.

- 'Replay' a conversation you've had and 'dance' with your hands in the shape of ears above your head. Put them in the position that fits the style of listening being done. Which of the ear gestures rarely gets used? Did you leave out a particular attitude of listening during that conversation? How might the conversation have gone if you had used it?

- Think of a remark someone made that got to you in one way or another. "Stop whining!" or "You'll just have to learn to live with it." If you like, write the remark down on a large piece of paper and place it in front of you. Then go through the four ear gestures in the same order as above and think, feel and speak your reaction while wearing each set of ears.

This transformation from jackal into giraffe could be described as an investigation into consciousness. To explain this, I want to make an exception and use the words 'good' and 'bad'. I don't usually do this, because during my upbringing, I learned to identify these words with what I 'should' and 'shouldn't' do, and that I would be rewarded or punished accordingly. It is necessary to make the distinction between good and bad in order to get past these ideas. To accomplish this, we then need to be completely honest with ourselves and delve into the 'evil' we can find in ourselves and in others. The purpose of this is to be able to be 'evil' with the 'evil' while keeping sight of the distinction between good and evil. In this way, we can as it were 'walk through the valley of the shadow of death' without allowing it to take us over completely.

'There's nowt as strange as folk' says the old adage. We know we can all sometimes be weak or lacking in awareness. By feeling into the depths of our souls, we can seek opportunities to meet our needs in other ways.

It is said that the giraffe can see from afar. His long neck, body and legs form a bridge we can use to cross over to new countries and new viewpoints. The giraffe sees not only far, but also sharply. In combination with his great height, this enables him to see right over the horizon; we could say into the other world: the spiritual world. There, he can see that we are all interconnected and how love facilitates this connection.

Like wolves and coyotes, jackals belong to the canine family of predators. The artist Joseph Beuys once allowed himself to be locked up for a week with a coyote. The coyote's response to Beuys' calm, patient attitude was recorded on both film and photograph. To begin with, the beast was anxious; he then became curious, approached, and finally, they were able to eat from the same bowl.

In the same way, the coyote or jackal in each of us can be tamed and can make respectful contact with another person's being as long as he feels safe.

6 We too can perform miracles

It really works. We listen to someone with giraffe ears and a moment later, he decides to talk to his girlfriend first before ending their relationship, instead of doing what he was planning to do, which was to send her an sms stating that he never wanted to see her again. Can this be called a miracle?

In my experience, miracles happen all the time when people have the courage to come out with their giraffe in jackal surroundings.

I enjoy reading Marianne Williamson's books. Her books are a supplement to and a kind of explanation of the Course in Miracles (an approach to enlightenment). When I started reading her books, I was a bit skeptical because I though miracles were exceptional things: recovering from a serious illness in the space of a day: the sort of thing I never imagined happening to me, let alone that I could bring about myself. The Course in Miracles turns out to be about a completely different kind of miracle. It's about special events in our lives which can sometimes have a transforming effect. This, I can work with. I might for instance think: "I feel like a bit of light relief. I've been sitting at this computer for hours". And then the doorbell rings and the little girl from next door, aged five, is standing there asking if I'd like to play with her. That's what I call a (small) miracle.

Before I go into this more deeply, I'd like to recount a folktale from East Africa, in which it becomes clear how the giraffe got his long neck by a miracle.

The giraffe's long neck

Once upon a time, long, long ago, when the giraffe's neck was just like the necks of all the other animals, their country was smitten by a terrible drought. The animals all gathered around the holes still containing a little water, to eat the last tufts of yellowing grass. Giraffe sighed and said to her friend, Rhino: "Just look at those green leaves, high up in the acacia tree. If only we could reach up there." "Grrr," growled Rhino, (a man of few words, was then and still is to this day): "Magician Man is clever – ask him what to do." So Giraffe went to Magician Man, who laughed and said: "Yes, I can help you with powerful herbs. Come back at sunrise tomorrow. The magical forces only work then." When the sun rose over the hills, Giraffe ate the herbs Magician Man had given her. Poor Rhino (who never remembered anything, never could and still can't to this day), overslept that day, there at the water-hole. Giraffe felt a tingling in her neck and a tingling in her legs and then, just like that, her legs and neck stretched out and - well, we all know what happened then. She walked, still a little wobbly, to the nearest group of acacia trees and since that day, she nibbles on the leaves of the acacia. If you look into her eyes, you can see how happy she is. (And Rhino is still angry; was then and still is to this day.)

This story is about a spectacular miracle, the like of which, as far as I know, can only happen in fairy tales. But whether spectacular or small (and by this I mean the miracles we witness in every day life), it doesn't do to sleep through the moment. Rhino slept through his opportunity and will always remain bitter. Giraffe was awake. She grasped her opportunity and now radiates joy.

Sometimes I'm too busy or too tired to register the subtle signals indicating that a miracle is happening. If a couple of clients cancel their appointments with me, I fail to realize that I now have time to attend to my belated administration. I may get angry if I think they've cancelled because they don't think their appointments with me are important enough. Or perhaps I'll feel insecure because I think I must be a bad coach if my clients cancel just like that.

There are days when I take it for granted that René has wizarded up a delicious meal again. I fail to appreciate that it's something special, to have met a man who loves cooking, so I can attend to my work or other things and still eat delicious, healthy food every day. I just sit down at table, eat my food and then return to my own thing.

In both cases, I am blind and deaf to the miracle of the concurrent circumstances, also referred to as synchronicity. I forget that life is actually one big miracle.

Sometimes I immediately see that life is smiling upon me. René comes home from town with stamps, just when I've used my last one. A sister who lives two hundred kilometers away, whom I haven't seen in three months, rings me up and sighs that she'd so love to see me. I tell her I'm going to be in her neighborhood for work the next day and we find a couple of hours in our busy diaries to meet for lunch.

This is surely miraculous. These are real miracles, 'coincidences' like these. When I am aware of them, I feel grateful. I yearn to experience more moments like these. I look to see what I can do myself or am already doing to make them possible. I think it has to do with connecting. Having a strong bond with both René and my sister, there is a greater likelihood that we will arrive at the same thoughts or that, as of their own accord, things will go as we would like them to. René and I experience this sort of thing quite often. I was recently in the town of Leiden, having lunch with a friend who recommended a certain CD to me. When I got home to Zutphen that evening, René had bought that very CD for me that same afternoon.

I sometimes have the same thing with other people. The more I feel connected at a certain moment with for instance my neighbor, my boss, the bus driver or whoever, the more likely it is that we'll complement one another or be thinking in the same direction.

I do odd jobs on a regular basis with a couple of friends from Amiel (previously mentioned in Chapter 2). We tune in with each other before we start, during the work and in between, during coffee or lunch breaks. We ask each other what we'd like to do next, how the work is coming along and how we are in ourselves as we work. The point is not so much the goal, but rather the personal and social process of our working together. Completing the work is an added bonus. The longer we work together, the more little miracles take place. Before I even realize I need a ladder, it's already beside me. We will all coincidentally step outside from our various workplaces at the very moment a van is arriving with a consignment of stones, so we can unload it together.

This is all about the giraffe attitude: an alertness whereby we continuously keep the others in our consciousness as we work. It's not a question of dividing our attention, but of being attentive to ourselves and what we are doing *and* to the presence and quality of presence of the people around us.

It requires more than just alertness to perform the kind of miracle in my example at the beginning of this chapter, where, after one conversation, someone decided to approach something with a more loving attitude. To contribute to the likelihood of this sort of miracle taking place, a more active giraffe attitude is necessary. It involves consciously deciding to welcome the jackal that presents itself; not fighting it; not judging it. We need to watch and listen. We need to pay attention to the feelings and needs hidden behind the jackal language. We can ask questions to increase clarity and make suggestions only if asked.

I think this is the attitude that Christ and the Buddha demonstrated for us, one which always seemed so far removed from my own. I thought I had to be fully enlightened before I could let go of my ego and feel totally at one with another person. Since I have got to know my inner giraffe, I have moments when I can feel and give that unconditional love. Christ had and has such an all-encompassing consciousness that he could and can empathize with all the pain and suffering felt by all beings. I believe that this Christ consciousness is growing in mankind. As long as we have not yet fully developed it, we are unable to feel at one with all people all the time. I suggest that we cherish the moments when we do experience this oneness.

I'd like to explain in another way what the connection might be between being a giraffe and experiencing miracles. I think it is a question of being plugged into the universe or not. When I'm in my jackal, I'm unplugged and when I'm in my giraffe, I'm plugged in.

Something just happened to me:

I was feeling good. I had just written one-and-a-half pages of this book, after which, for a change of scenery, I was chatting to René while I folded the washing. I walked back into my study and the following thought flashed through my mind: tomorrow, I'm going to print my pamphlet, so today, people can still phone and plan a workshop with me, and I'll be able to include it in the pamphlet.

Ten minutes later, the phone rang. A spiritual centre in the north of Holland was on the line wanting to know if I'd be prepared to run a two-day workshop for them in the spring.

Apparently, we were both plugged into the universe and the connection was easy to make. If I had been unplugged,

I may have wrestled with a passage in my book for hours, and deleted the few lines I had written. I could have gone into the kitchen in frustration and squabbled with René about his buying an electric drill, meanwhile eating half the contents of the biscuit box. Back in my study, I might have thought: "I've postponed printing my pamphlet for a week now and not one single extra workshop has come in. You see? They just don't want me."

It would have been very tricky for the spiritual centre to find me in the middle of that little black cloud.

And now a few stories about how you can influence other people's happiness once you've found your way into your giraffe: what you can contribute in the way of everyday miracles.

Your neighbors are taking you to court because, according to them, you have planted some trees on their ground. You go to see them and you give them the opportunity to get it all off their chests. You say you're curious to hear the judge's decision and that you are not thinking of taking it any further. On the day of the hearing, the neighbor's wife comes round to ask if you'd like a lift in their car. You depart, chatting away merrily.

Your son comes home with a red cheek. He has been hit by the father of one of his classmates. You seat him on your lap and allow him to tell his story. You go to these people's house and talk to the father about his problems at work and about bringing up his children. At the end of the conversation, the father invites you and your family round for a barbecue at the weekend.

I read the following in a newspaper. A woman was driving her car along a country road with her daughter when she was hit by another car. She was seriously injured herself and her daughter died in hospital. The driver of the other car, another woman, was unharmed. She visited the injured woman several times in the hospital. And they continued to meet when the injured woman had returned home. They were a great support to each other as they each worked through the effects of the accident.

I was deeply impressed by these two women's ability to stay in connection. It may be that one of the two was the first to act in a giraffe-like way and that the other's jackal sailed along in her wake, changing into a giraffe herself. It may also be that both took on a giraffe attitude from the start.

So when we behave as giraffes, it can have a miraculous effect on other people's behavior. Miracles can also have more to do with changes in ourselves. Taking the reins into our own hands and taking responsibility for meeting our own needs can change our lives completely. The jackal we thereby transform is the victim jackal. I will give a couple of examples of this too.

An older woman lives in an old people's home. She is alone much of the time and complains that no-one ever comes to visit her. She complains to the staff and to the visitors who do come occasionally and are happy when they can leave again. She then arrives at the idea of visiting the other residents herself. After a few months, she has changed into a cheerful lady with a busy diary.

My two daughters and my son like going out to bars and parties. I once heard them tell each other that they couldn't understand the way some young people whine such a lot. They just hang around the bar waiting for something to happen: "When's something going to happen for a change? Why does everyone always come so late? The music is lousy again tonight." My children shrug their shoulders when they hear this sort of remark. They are never troubled by boring parties, because they make the party themselves. They make sure they have a good time. And if they don't feel like going to a party, they stay at home.

From the stories (or miracles if you like) you've read about in this chapter, it will be clear that we can influence our happiness ourselves. Happiness is not for sale, but we can have an influence on it.

His long slim legs give the giraffe the ability to stay in balance and to stand firmly on the ground. With his long neck, he reaches up to the heavens. You can feel what this is like if you stand with your legs apart, and place your feet firmly on the ground. Lift the crown of your head towards the sky and make yourself tall. Feel the power of your self. You need this power to stand up for what is true and important for you. Only if you stand firm can you be open and listen to and feel what is true and important for another. Then you needn't be afraid of being trodden underfoot. You are confident that you matter.

In jackal society the social unit is that of a monogamous pair which defends its territory from other pairs. These territories are defended by vigorously chasing intruding rivals away and marking landmarks around the territory with urine and faeces.

I guess this is done out of a need for safety. When I myself feel unsafe I also intend to mark my borders clearly. I can do this without respect for other people's feelings and needs by just letting my 'shit' out whether they want to hear it or not. If the jackal in the other person does the same, the result is a dirty mess.

If we would invite our giraffes in, they would see our need for safety. Then our giraffes could meet at the borders we created by putting out the landmarks, connect with each other and maybe invite each other to cross the border.

7 Jackaling at other people: what it says about us

What do we do more often? Jackal about ourselves or jackal about others? My initial impulse is to say: "Jackal about others".

My jackal would tend to say the same. If I'm not feeling at one with the world, I prefer to blame the man who rang me this morning, the weather, my partner, an article in the paper. There doesn't even have to be a direct connection. I just think of the politicians who don't listen but just try to convince us that they're right, of the child labor going on in the world, or of the luxury items the rich people of the western world spend their money on. My jackal is always lurking and given half a chance, he embarks on one of his tirades. Not only does he run people into the ground, he also builds them up: "That film star is wonderful." "My children are doing so well." "What a fantastic book." With no difficulty whatever, I'll praise anyone to the skies. The jackal classifies, judges and compares.

I see and hear jackals around me expressing themselves fully and freely too. On the street, in the train, when I occasionally watch the television. They are exuberantly present.

This is actually quite logical of course. For thousands of years, jackal language has been passed on from father to son, from mother to daughter. Whatever happens, someone has to take the blame for it and every success has to be attributed to someone.

I now notice, with people who are involved in becoming conscious, how they gradually discover that they too are full of judgments about themselves. Their judgments of other people and of matters outside of themselves turn out to be reflections of the judgments they have of themselves. They were in the habit of denying the discontent and insecurity they had about their own thoughts and deeds and to shout them down by criticizing others. Once they slowly start to drop their judgments of others, enormous amounts of self-criticism are laid bare. They see themselves as worthless, and have very little self-confidence. A woman once told me she used to wake up every morning with a feeling of shame. She was ashamed because she did far too little for other people and she was always tired. She was ashamed of being alive.

If we were able to work out how many people suffer from a lack of self-worth and self-confidence, we could speak in terms of an epidemic.

Does this mean we might as well stop doing endless consciousness-raising courses? Running others down is after all so much easier, and less painful too.

I'm sure you understand where this is going. I see jackaling at ourselves as an in-between phase between blaming the outside world for everything we experience as unpleasant and embracing that world. In this in-between phase, we learn to see and meet ourselves after which we are able to meet other people. We learn to see our darker side, the one we have hidden from ourselves in the shadows. It is necessary to shine the light into our shadows if we want to get to know ourselves fully. We may be frightened by what we find. We want to see it, but we have difficulty accepting what we see, and we tend to judge ourselves. So it can be useful to have a giraffe on hand to listen to the jackal, whether in thought, on a card in our purse, or as a little cuddly toy in our bag.

I have discovered that I find it easier to get to know my shadows through other people. So I start off for example, by mentally saying: "What a stupid idiot" or: "What an arrogant jerk" about somebody else. I have read how I can progress from this point in Byron Katie's work. She asks us amongst other things to examine whether what we say is actually true.

Later on, she asks us to say the sentence in the first person. So with the above examples, it becomes: "I'm such a stupid idiot" or: "I'm such an arrogant jerk". This reminds me of a saying I heard more than once during my childhood: "It takes one to know one." If I had been calling someone all sorts of names and they said this to me, to say that I didn't like it would be an understatement. In fact, I would become even more enraged than I had been in the first place, if that were possible. I now realize that this was probably because I knew it was true. Everything I say about someone else says something about me. I too am sometimes stupid or arrogant, or at least, I sometimes do things that might be judged in those words.

I now need to ask my giraffe to join in with this conversation. If I don't, I will land myself with a great big judgment about myself. This will not make me happy nor will anyone else be served by it. But my giraffe can help me to see which aspect of myself I think is stupid or arrogant. What have I said or done? I did it in order to meet a need. What need was that? How was I feeling when I didn't get what I longed for? Suppose the need was for recognition. What other opportunities do I have for gaining that recognition?

I hereby invite you to examine your own judgments and self-judgments in this way. Once all this is clear to you, take the time to mourn your imperfections. Smile and know that anyone who was to fall in love with you now (or the person who is in love with you already) accepts you fully, including your imperfections. If you would like to be completely independent of other people for your self-worth, fall in love with yourself.

I once went on a clowning course with Roelant de Vletter, a well-known Dutch clown. On the third day, we sat on the ground in a circle. Roelant asked us to take turns getting up, walking over to someone, making a judgment about them, sitting down again and making the same judgment about ourselves. It was truly astonishing.

I went up to a woman and said: "I think you're the centre of attention far too much of the time and that irritates the hell out of me". I sat down again, shut my eyes and yes, as if of its own accord, an image of myself came up as my brothers and sisters had seen me during my childhood. They thought I was always seeking attention and that I shouldn't. I should be more modest. I had internalized this opinion and thought that attention-seeking was bad and if I did it, I should be ashamed. I put the sentence into the first person and said to myself: "I think I want to be the centre of attention far too much of the time". I got in touch with my longing to be seen and the pleasure that it affords me even now, as an adult. I wept about how I had stuck the label of 'shameful' on it, and forgave myself for having done it. That same afternoon, I performed an improvisation with the woman I had criticized. We both enjoyed it enormously.

I had separated the judgment 'I shouldn't' and the fact 'I like to be the centre of attention' from each other. I could now shamelessly enjoy getting attention, thereby fulfilling my need to be seen.

Not only when we run someone into the ground are we saying something about the judgments we have of ourselves. When we admire someone too, we do it because we recognize and cherish the same qualities in ourselves, even when we don't believe or don't yet believe that we can be as scintillating or as caring and considerate as the person we find so wonderful.

I remember a number of meetings in my life in which this admiration played a role. I would see all sorts of qualities in a certain person and feel grateful for the experience. I would feel strong and happy. If I told the person, it would turn out that he or she felt the same in relation to me. So I would admire the qualities in the other person, that I was less able to see in myself, while the other person would see similar qualities in me, but again less in him self. We had looked into the mirror, but we had forgotten we were looking at ourselves. We thought we were looking through a window at each other.

I have a friend I admire for the clarity and care with which she expresses herself. I also like the way she listens to me and reflects back what she's heard, packaged just slightly differently from how I said it, which makes it easier for me to accept myself. I have the following image of her: a radiant, powerful woman who excels in her work as a coach for both individuals and company communication processes. She herself felt insecure about her work as a trainer. She thinks she doesn't have enough training or experience. She admires me for my determination. I write books in which I express myself so clearly and carefully! She enjoys the way I listen to her and reflect back what I've heard, packaged just slightly differently from how she said it, making it easier for her to accept herself. Now where have I heard this before?

My friend and I put each other up on pedestals. Our jackals compare themselves with each other and each sees the other as wiser and better than him self. But in this way, my friend and I stimulate each other too, especially as we now know we are talking about our own qualities seen in the other. At first this was unconscious but it's now conscious too. We enjoy the contact because we invite our giraffes to empathize with the negative self-images rearing their heads from time to time and to see the qualities in the other as well as in ourselves.

This makes our relationship beneficial to both of us. I am grateful to my jackal for praising this woman and I'm grateful to my giraffe for showing me the difference between praising someone's qualities and enjoying someone's qualities and recognizing them in myself. Both of these starting points together have given me a fruitful and enjoyable friendship.

The giraffe dares to show his vulnerability. To be able to drink, he has to maneuver his forelegs wide apart, step by careful step. From this position, he cannot immediately run away, should that be necessary. This demands courage and trust. We need courage and trust too, to say what we are feeling, to make a request instead of a demand, with the risk that the other will say no. We may think the world will come to an end if we stop manipulating or trying to turn our environment or even the world to our hand. The jackal in us is frightened of showing his vulnerability. The giraffe recognizes and acknowledges his fear and takes action anyway.

Every jackal family has its own call and jackals listen only to the call of their own family, ignoring those of others. This reminds me of the way we people can collect groups of like-minded people around us. Within our action group, political party, religious community, group of friends, we more or less agree with each other on most points. We compare our group with other political parties etc. We are of course, always the best. They are stupid, can't handle money, don't get what the world is about. We do of course, because we're more intelligent. I think most conflicts could be avoided if we were to create space for listening not only to the call of our own 'family' but also to that of other families.

8 Jackal and giraffe language

You have by now probably got a fair picture of the personality and the characteristics of the giraffe and the jackal. For the sake of order and clarity and especially for those who like tables and diagrams, in this chapter, I have made a table showing a number of giraffe and jackal characteristics followed by examples of speech and sentences they tend to use.

First the characteristics: the list is incomplete, so feel free to add any characteristics you think are important.

I'd like to invite you to recognize each characteristic as one you have in yourself too: those of the giraffe and those of the jackal. You may like at each point to imagine a situation in which your behavior was as described. When do you observe with an open mind? When have you tried to be better than someone else? Don't forget to enjoy both.

JACKAL	GIRAFFE
Concentrating on differences and comparing them, leading to loneliness.	Maintaining the intention of connecting by realizing that we are all one. We are all people and in that sense, equal.
Indifference and/or heartlessness, with or without supplying explanations and solutions.	Compassion, the ability to empathize, to be with what is.
Punishing, harboring grudges and thoughts of revenge.	Forgiving, letting go and making space for love.
Interpreting, allowing our thoughts to run away with us, away from the now.	Witnessing without prejudice, using all the senses actively. In this way, staying in the now.
Manipulating, trying to steer and alter.	Bringing acceptance and trust into our thinking.
Concentrating on what we think about something and how we can get our way.	Being creative about fulfilling our needs. Taking action ourselves or making open requests.
Coercing or demanding or whining when our needs are not met.	Please add to this list any giraffe or jackal character traits you come across in yourself or others which do not appear on the above list.
_____	_____
_____	_____
_____	_____
_____	_____
_____	_____
_____	_____

Please add to this list any giraffe or jackal character traits you come across in yourself or others which do not appear on the above list.

The differences between jackal and giraffe language can be summed up as follows:

Loving from a position of trust

and

Hating from a position of fear

Connection

and

Alienation

In everything we say, we can find one if not several of the above-mentioned qualities. If not expressed in the words, it will be expressed in the tone of voice, the psychological attitude or physical posture adopted while speaking them. On the next page, you will find some sentences and conversations in which the giraffe and the jackal are apparent in the words.

To start with, there is a series of examples of jackal and giraffe sayings alongside the four elements of the Nonviolent Communication model.

OBSERVING	
The jackal interprets, judges, generalizes, labels and trivializes, saying:	The giraffe observes and says:
I can see you don't understand.	I see you raising your eyebrows.
You've left the door open again.	The door is open.
You haven't had a wash this morning, you're a disgrace.	I can smell something I don't like.
Haven't you finished that little bit of homework yet?	I can see you're writing. How far have you got with your homework?
People just don't understand me.	He said he didn't understand me.
FEELING	
The jackal, who quasi-feels (he interprets while thinking he is sharing what he feels), says:	The giraffe, who feels, says:
I feel attacked.	I feel uneasy when you say that.
I feel there's something not right.	I feel unsure.
I don't feel seen.	I feel sad because I get the impression that you don't see how it is for me.
It feels as if everyone's out to get me.	I'm afraid and I feel unsafe.
I feel understood.	I'm happy and I feel connected to you.

NEEDING	
The jackal, who takes his strategies for needs, says:	**The giraffe, who expresses his needs, says:**
It's time we made love again.	I want some intimacy.
I want my boss to recognize my qualities.	I would so love my qualities to be recognized.
My body needs meat.	My body needs food.
You give such bad lessons, I'm learning nothing.	I want to learn.
To respect each other, we have to let each other finish talking.	Mutual respect is very important to me.
MAKING REQUESTS	
The jackal, who demands or orders, says:	**The giraffe, who makes requests, says:**
Repeat what I just said!	Could you tell me what you heard me say?
You pour the tea.	Will you pour the tea or shall I?
Could you call me back? (When there is no room for a 'no'.)	Could you call me back? (When either 'yes' or 'no' are OK.)
Take your shoes off first.	Would you take off your shoes and put them in the corridor?
If you don't go, I'm not going either.	I'd love you to come with me. Do you want to?

In the following conversations, Aj is person A's jackal and Ag is person A's giraffe. Person B's jackal is Bj and his or her giraffe is Bg.

Let's start with two jackals.

Aj: Sir, if you don't turn your car round immediately, I'm going to call the police.

Bj: Well, I'm not going to, because I want to go in that direction. If you'll just let me pass, I'll be out of your way.

Aj: I'm trying to get my work done here! *(guiding two jug-
gernaut trucks)* Now turn round or I'll kick your rotten
car to bits.

Bj: Don't you threaten me like that. Call the police if you
like, and we'll soon see what's what.

And now a giraffe who can't handle the jackal in the other
and becomes a jackal too.

Ag: There's still half a lemon. Maybe it would be nice in the
fruit salad. Would you like to use it for that?

Bj: Why do you always have to stick your nose into everything I do in the kitchen?

Ag: *(thinks: she's needing her autonomy and some space while
she's cooking and is feeling irritated)* OK, I won't get in
your way.

Bj: You are in my way! Whenever I'm trying to concentrate
on a recipe, you come and stand by me and ask all sorts
of questions. Leave me alone!

Aj: *(it has now become too much for him and he goes on the
defensive)* You think I'm doing it deliberately. I'm only
trying to help.

And this is how a giraffe sounds, even when the other remains a jackal.

Ag: Tomorrow is Uncle Pete's and Aunt Karin's wedding. I
know you want to go out this evening. What time are
you planning to get home?

Bj: How can I know that?

Ag: Am I right in thinking you don't want to say what time
you'll be home because you don't know how much fun
it will be yet?

Bj: Don't nag. I don't want to talk about it.

Ag: Are you looking forward to the wedding tomorrow?

Bj: What a stupid question. Of course not. A whole day of people moaning on about "How old are you now?" and "How are you doing at school?" And that awful music.

Ag: I can hear it's not your idea of a good party. I really appreciate you agreeing to go, even when you don't think you'll enjoy it. I do like to see the whole family together, so to me, you belong there.

Bj: Stop trying to butter me up. You'll have me in tears any minute now.

Ag: I hope you enjoy this evening, anyway. And that I'll be able to wake you up at eight o'clock in the morning.

During a conversation, a jackal can turn into a giraffe.

Aj: Where are those documents I asked you for? I haven't heard a thing from you all week and it's just not good enough.

Bg: It sounds like you really need them?

Aj: Yes, that's what I said, isn't it? I have to hold that presentation tomorrow and I need the information I asked you for. I really feel let down.

Bg: Have you been waiting for my response and support all week and the presentation's tomorrow? If I were in your shoes, I'd be feeling pretty nervous. Are you?

Ag: *(realizing she has been heard and now able to make contact with her feelings)* Yes, I certainly am. The whole Board is going to be listening. That's pretty scary, so I want to be thoroughly prepared. Can you get that information to me now?

Bg: I'll mail it to you right away. I'm sorry it's been such a long wait for you. I'd have wished you a more relaxed preparation time. Would you like to know why I didn't get in touch with you?

Ag: Well, I'm glad I spoke to you in time. Yes, why didn't you respond to my request?

Bg: I was in bed with a heavy dose of bronchitis and today's my first day back at the office.

Ag: That can't have been much fun. Well, all the best with catching up on your work. I won't hold you up any longer.

In a conversation between two jackals, one of them can decide to bring his giraffe into play. Here is an example in three versions. In the first, both A and B remain jackals. They both get bogged down in old patterns and for the rest of the evening, either snipe at each other or keep a tight-lipped silence. Then there is a version in which A calls in the aid of his giraffe followed by a version in which B does so.

In the first one, both A and B begin as giraffes, but tempers flare as soon as A is triggered by B's unwitting answer.

Ag: That pianist was a real Russian.

Bg: The pianist, did you say?

Aj: Yes, who else would I mean?

Bj: Don't overreact! I just asked a question.

Aj: Well don't be so stupid. There was only one Russian in the whole concert and that was the pianist, so who else would I mean?

Bj: I just hadn't heard you properly. It can happen. There's no need to blow up at me like that.

Aj: But it happens so often. I say something and you don't hear it properly. Instead of just thinking what I might mean for a moment, you immediately ask questions. Use your common sense for a change!

Bj: Oh come on now. Don't get all worked up about nothing. I don't feel like being shouted at. So stuff it! *(followed by the BANG of a door being slammed shut)*

What these jackals need is for someone to give their ears a gentle tug so they stop bickering and realize they have been triggered. A takes the lead and tugs on B's ears.

Ag: That pianist was a real Russian.
Bg: The pianist, did you say?
Aj: Yes, who else would I mean?
Bj: Don't overreact! I just asked a question.
Ag: Did my reaction startle you?
Bj: Yes, of course it did. I asked the question because I didn't hear you properly and you get so irritated. As if I've done something wrong.
Ag: You'd enjoy having the opportunity to check if you've heard right?
Bg: Yes, then I'd have the idea it was accepted. I'd like it if you'd just say: 'Yes, the pianist.' And then go on with what you were saying, because I am curious about that. Why did you think he was such a Russian?

And finally, the version in which B becomes a giraffe first.

Ag: That pianist was a real Russian.
Bg: The pianist, did you say?
Aj: Yes, who else would I mean?
Bg: Are you cross because I didn't understand you?
Aj: I don't care whether you understand me or not, but when you ask stupid questions like that, it's really irritating. You can work it out for yourself that I'm talking about the pianist. He was the only Russian in the whole concert.
Bg: So you'd like it if what you say is heard and if that's the subject of conversation?
Aj: Yes, I want to talk about the Russian and not have to explain what I mean.
Bg: I get the impression you'd like to be taken seriously and you want people to be genuinely interested in what you say.

Ag: Yes. If you say: "The pianist?" I think you doubt there was only one Russian. I think you must think I'm stupid. I realize now it was my thoughts that made me angry and not what you said. Thanks for paying attention to my irritation.

What we could also do in this last example, is to psychologize. In his past, A has probably often heard the message that he is stupid. So as soon as he thinks anyone thinks he's stupid, he goes on the attack. B immediately thinks she has done something wrong, so as a child, she was probably punished or criticized for her mistakes.

This psychologizing is not necessary to restore the connection between these two. In Nonviolent Communication, we look for the feelings and needs behind the jackal reaction. And these feelings and needs are here in the present.

Giraffes have a very mobile under-lip which, in relation to the upper lip, moves as our thumb moves in relation to our fingers. This is very useful. To think up real giraffe words and sentences, we sometimes need considerable agility. For years, we have been brought up with jackal language, so it's all very new. When we have only just begun to learn this new language, we may start stuttering and stammering. It may help to think of the giraffe's lip mobility coming to our rescue in this tricky situation.

Jackal pups stay in the den for around the first three months. From then on, they learn to hunt. On practice hunts, the prey is chased until the moment when it can be killed, and is then allowed to escape. It was after all, just an exercise. This reminds me of the dry runs I do when I'm trying to get some clarity about what's bothering me. I let my jackals have their say: the blamer, the judge, the victim, the comparer and anyone else who wants to chip in. I keep all this to myself. I don't say anything to the person the blaming and judging is aimed at. I then look at what feelings and unmet needs are behind my judging and blaming. And it is with these feelings and needs that I go to the person who has activated the jackals in me. Or not. It is sometimes enough just to do this self-examination. If I succeed in doing this work in time, as long as my jackals are still pups, I am able to keep them under control. If I ignore them and wait until they are fully grown, it becomes a lot more difficult and they tend to go in for the kill.

9 Social change

Suppose we are enthusiastic about what we have read in this book and would like to integrate it into our lives. Suppose we choose to use Nonviolent Communication to learn giraffe language. This would mean a change in how we look at ourselves and how we respond to our environment. This could be viewed as a spiritual change, an alteration at the level of the soul.

Is it not so that by beginning with ourselves, we can initiate change in our surroundings? In fact, I think social change is only ever brought about by individual change. And the only person responsible for that is the individual.

As individuals, we can try to force change and go and try to convince everyone that Nonviolent Communication is *the* solution to all problems. With a lot of promises and a good advertising campaign, we may get lots of people involved. What we are doing then is placing one method above others because we think it is better. This, in my opinion, leads to separation, and not to connection. This approach can come from a longing for peace and unity for all but can have the reverse effect. I think it is a tragic way of trying to achieve unity. It's a method from which the spiritual aspect of Nonviolent Communication is missing. It comes from a deliberated urge to change the world by establishing a new system. The umpteenth new system.

This conviction, this wanting to capture the whole world in *one* system can be seen in religious and spiritual organizations. Religious wars are an example of this. In my life, I sometimes experience the following:

I go to a lecture. For the ensuing months, I receive weekly e-mails with invitations to workshops and several recruiting phone-calls asking if I would like to become a student. I am reminded of my responsibility to make a contribution to world peace. And I don't feel free. I need space to make my own choices.

Even more painful is when a friend tries to persuade me to read certain books, to join a certain group or to follow a certain diet because it would be better for me and the world. I experience this as intrusive and as an attempt to limit my freedom. I like to decide for myself where I want to focus my attention. For me, it is a value (as in norms and values, but without the norms) that everyone is free to choose his or her own path of development and that we respect each others paths.

How can we (and by 'we' I mean those of us who trust in the power of Nonviolent Communication and who want to put our efforts into spreading it world-wide) bring more nonviolence to the world without recruitment campaigns? After all, Marshall Rosenberg urges us, from this position of trust, to put our efforts into social change. What I understand by this is a kind of spirituality integrating into all aspects of society. This spirituality of connectivity can find its way into our society along all sorts of canals. Nonviolent Communication may be the way, or it may be another way. It doesn't matter. So the method by which ministries, organizations and companies are approached about Nonviolent Communication has to be different from the method I have just described. It needs to be presented in the form of an invitation, in harmony with an already existing wish.

I advise starting by approaching people who are already curious, who have the idea that Nonviolent Communication is what the world needs and who want to investigate how they can do their share. By making the ideas of Nonviolent Communication known, by informally writing about it for newspapers and magazines, by talking about it on television, by providing information to those in top positions, it will become clear who wants to be approached about Nonviolent Communication. The emphasis here is on 'informal': no strings attached, no obligation. At each first meeting, ideas and expectations are shared in freedom. Each meeting is a tuning in to each others feelings and needs with connection as the aim, not just winning a new client.

I notice myself that workshops I plan anonymously (I find a good location, set a date, advertise and wait) frequently attract few if any people. The workshops that fill up of their own accord are organized by enthusiastic people. Their enthusiasm is catching within their circle of friends, school, company or spiritual centre.

Training is not everyone's path to growth. Those enthusiastic about Nonviolent Communication can use it at any juncture, creating an example of their own communication. By listening with giraffe ears to measures being considered, to assignments and bills of law, and by making our comments about what we would like to do differently in giraffe language, we can influence the organization of companies, education and the political climate. Everyone who wants to can take part in this, whether they are ordinary citizens communicating with the school board, working for the personnel department of a company or Members of Parliament.

The question we can examine here is: how can we maintain freedom within social structures? I offer the following ideas as possible answers to this question. By allowing everyone his or her freedom of thought and doing a giraffe dance around apparently opposing thoughts and plans. By talking about other ways of realizing plans – ways benefitting everyone and not only those who have thought up the plan, or the people in the same party or company. By, as far as possible, formulating rules together in order thereafter to choose in freedom to live by them, whether we agree with them or are merely not against them. By attaching more importance to living together as free individuals than to structures held together by rules, and by punishment when these are broken.

Arriving at a decision with the aid of the 'no objection' method is used in amongst other methods, sociocracy. Sociocracy is a form of management which assumes the equality of individuals.

It is not necessary to set up a new school or movement called Nonviolent Communication. Nonviolent Communication fits into all existing movements. Every school can become a Rosenberg school, every political party a Rosenberg party, every company a Rosenberg company. This is possible if the people involved in the school, party or company become conscious of their jackal and their giraffe, listen from their giraffe to the jackal and translate his words into feelings and needs. This applies too to the media, religious institutions, families and neighborhoods. And to prisons, hospitals and sports clubs. In fact, to any place where people come together.

I find it a challenge, in fields where the jackal has the upper hand, such as in theaters of war, and in my experience, often in politics and the business world, to shake the giraffe awake so that the balance between jackal and giraffe can be redressed.

I'd like to offer some clarity about where you can get guidance on learning to communicate nonviolently. There are companies that specialize in teaching and carrying out the ideas of Nonviolent Communication. There are circles of people on their way towards integrating it into their lives. Traveling the path together helps to combine forces and increase concentration. I am aware that other names are sometimes used for Nonviolent Communication such as Compassionate Communication, Communicating from the Heart and Open-Hearted Communication.

There is an international network, the Center for Nonviolent Communication. This CNVC has the aim of being an open organization, open to all who want to learn and spread Nonviolent Communication.

An example of a country in which the social change I am talking about here has gained enormous momentum is Brazil.

A few years ago, Marshall Rosenberg's book was bought and read for the first time by a Brazilian: Dominic Barter. In November 2006, the work of a group of active practitioners of Nonviolent Communication led to an official, permanent Peace Council becoming part of the department of legislation of the Ministry of Justice.

Since then Barter has worked on a worldwide network of Restorative Justice, which is an approach to justice that focuses on the needs of the victims and the offenders, as well as the involved community, instead of satisfying abstract legal principles or punishing the offender.

Since the year 2000, on the advice of the Ministry of Education, Israel has had a schools' program for the prevention of violence. Workshops in Nonviolent Communication are provided for educational supervisors, teachers and parents and the number of 'giraffes' is growing.

Further examples can be found on the website of the International Center for Nonviolent Communication, www. cnvc.org.

Social change is also to be found in areas where no-one has ever heard of Nonviolent Communication, or at least, where those specific words are not used. I'd like to mention a few projects to show that using our giraffe is a universal phenomenon even if the people doing it are not aware that I call it giraffe activity.

I'm thinking for example of Micro-credit, a concept whereby small amounts of sometimes no more than 50 euros are lent to people with no work and/or no money to live from. The man who started this up in the 1970's is Muhammad Yunus. He was awarded the Nobel Prize for it in 2006. To lend money to someone and have no idea whether you will get it back demands trust and choosing love above security. I think the people who receive this money experience more support and respect than if it was donated to them. When people donate money, they have actually already given up on you: "You can't look after yourself and you'll never be able to. You are and will remain dependent on the generosity of others." Yunus is of the opinion that charity is not a good basis for relationships between people. He thinks that if we want to solve the problem of poverty, we have to enable people to build their own lives. If people are given loans, I think it is a stimulus to honor the trust and respect inherent in the loan. In practice, it turns out that indeed, with micro-credit, both the interest and the principal are more often paid back on time than with loans from commercial banks.

It was no mean task for Yunus to gain support for his approach from banks and industry. The jackals around him responded to it with criticism, fear and mistrust. It took enormous determination on his part to prove that micro-credit was a success for both borrowers and lenders.

The Dutch princess Maxima has been an enthusiastic advocate of micro-credit for years.

Another place where the giraffes have risen is in South Africa when, after Apartheid had been dismantled, the Committee for Truth and Reconciliation was installed. This committee was set up after the black population, which had previously been oppressed, came into power in 1994. Jackal acts of revenge against the white oppressors might well have been expected. But instead of this, during the process of Truth and Reconciliation, victims and perpetrators listened to each other's stories. What then happened was that the victims forgave the perpetrators and the perpetrators were able to forgive themselves. They all freed themselves from hate, a giraffe act in its purest form.

In Rwanda, where in 1994, during the war between the Hutus and the Tutsis, about twelve per cent of the total population was massacred, it was not so much a question of finding out the truth. Everyone knew what had happened. There, people chose for *gacaca* (pronounced ga-cha-cha). This means that victims and suspected perpetrators meet each other in the presence of other members of the community. They speak of what was done to them or of what they themselves have done. The victims are given complete freedom to express themselves, seek support and cry (giraffe). They are not allowed to seek revenge (jackal). The punishments dealt out to the guilty enable them to work with others on rebuilding the country.

This process does not perhaps immediately lead to forgiveness. It does require the will to connect and to continue living together, although we are not always conscious of this. This desire is present in all mankind.

One person who was able to forgive is Immaculée Ilibagiza. In her book 'The Pain of Freedom', she describes how, after wrestling with huge pain and grief, she visits the murderer of her mother and brothers in prison. She forgives him. The guard who escorts the man to her is furious at her and speechless with surprise. When he asks: "Why did you forgive him?" she answers: "I have nothing to offer but forgiveness."

Her suffering has put her in touch with a power she does not keep to herself. She contributes to social change by working, in 2006, with the Commission for Sustainable Development of the United Nations. Through the Left to Tell Charitable Fund, she has already found foster homes for more than sixty orphans in Rwanda.

When I read about this I felt happy, as I do now as I write. Fortunately, I hear about this sort of giraffe act with increasing frequency, taking place all over the world. This gives me hope for the future.

Another thing that gives me hope is the influence this growth of the giraffe has on human behavior. I mean 'behavior' in the broadest sense of the word. The following are changes I see in my own behavior. As often as possible, I eat organic and vegetarian food. I wear clothes made of natural materials, preferably made in an environment-friendly and people-friendly way. I am sparing with energy, at home, in my choice of fuel for my car and in my manner of driving. I treat plants and animals with respect. I no longer kill flies and mosquitoes, but catch them in a glass and escort them outside. We can communicate non-violently with everything that exists: with people, animals, plants and the earth. If I hear a mosquito whining around my head at night, I ask it to stay away until I have fallen asleep. Then he is welcome to bite me gently here and there. For people with an allergic reaction to mosquito-bites, a mosquito-net can be handy too.

Where I think of it, I put my giraffe to work on all sorts of little tasks I perform. Dealing with a paper-jam in my printer, changing the batteries for the back light on my bicycle, cleaning my house; everything runs more smoothly if I am inwardly connected and cooperate with the matter at hand.

The growing number of people interacting with their environments more consciously and with more respect also contributes to social change. More and more organizations and industries are responding to people's wish to live with respect for everything around them. A magazine such as Ode, which is full of conscious, peace-loving initiatives, has, in ten years time, grown into a periodical with a worldwide distribution, printing more than 100,000 copies per issue.

Giraffes have hooves bigger than our heads. They use them to hold off aggressors. They do not, themselves, attack. Their hooves are used only to defend themselves. The giraffe in us is not always entirely gentle either. He uses his strength and his power to protect himself and others, and to prevent violence from being used. It is sometimes necessary to get a good hold on someone to prevent him from beating us up before we've had the chance to look for his feelings and needs, the triggers for his violent behavior. If, out of fear or fury, we grab him so hard that his ribs break, we have crossed the border into jackal-hood.

Giraffes never use their hooves to attack their own sort. If we were able to follow their example, there would be an end to all inter-human violence in the world. We often think in terms of different nations, races, cultures, political parties, but in fact we all belong to the same race: the human race.

During his life, General Charles de Gaulle was loved by many, but also hated by many. There were various attacks made on him. One of them is described by Frederick Forsyth in his book 'The Day of Jackal'. The attack on the general in this book was planned by a merciless English hired killer, completely devoid of emotion.

This is the kind of jackal I find very hard to love. It is also the kind that needs love the most.

10 Other authors on the jackal and the giraffe

Taking political action is one way of contributing to social change. Writing is another. I am happy that more and more books about Nonviolent Communication are published. And I realize that all the books about love and spiritual insight are in fact also describing the path from jackal-hood to giraffe-hood.

In this chapter, there are ten quotations from various authors, each followed by a few words about how they, to my mind, relate to the giraffe and the jackal.

A miracle worker interprets all loveless actions as a cry for love. When looked at in this light, someone who closes off his heart to you can no longer hurt you. Because it is not that the person has closed off his heart to you that hurts, but the instinctive reaction of closing off your own heart too. Pray for those who have failed you and the pain you are suffering will turn into peace. *
Marinanne Williamson, *The Gift of Change*

A miracle worker (giraffe) interprets all loveless actions (jackal behavior) as a cry for love. When looked at in this light, someone who closes off his heart to you (jackal) can no longer hurt you. Because it is not that the person has closed off his heart to you that hurts, but the instinctive reaction of closing off your own heart too (your own jackal). Pray (giraffe) for those who have failed you and the pain you are suffering will turn into peace.

The more I clung to my children and to what I expected of life, the more threatening life became. The more I learned to let go, to allow my plans and expectations to go their own way and to accept what we came across on our path, the safer life became for us. *
William Martin, *The Parent's Tao Te Ching*

The more I clung to my children and to what I expected of life (jackal attempts to fulfill my need for safety), the more threatening life became. The more I learned to let go, to allow my plans and expectations to go their own way and to accept what we came across on our path (giraffe way of meeting my needs for safety and trust), the safer life became for us.

A peaceful way of resolving a conflict is by showing respect for your opponent. The mistake often made is to demonstrate power rather than respect. The respect is beaten into us. There is another way. I have more than once heard from professional negotiators that seemingly insurmountable obstacles can disappear as snow before the sun when the parties concerned really get the idea that they are being treated equally. *
Deepak Chopra, *Peace is the Way*

A peaceful way of resolving a conflict is by showing respect for your opponent (demonstrating the intention of being a giraffe). The mistake often made is to demonstrate power rather than respect. The respect is beaten into us (showing respect becomes a jackal demand in this way). There is another way. I have more than once heard from professional negotiators that seemingly insurmountable obstacles can disappear as snow before the sun when the parties concerned really get the idea that they are being treated equally (when the giraffe respects both parties, this leads to a cooperative giraffe attitude in all involved).

When a thought arises, do not judge it. Merely observe it, as soon as a consciousness dawns in you that is actively involved in considering every kind of thought, every sort of feeling. In this way, you can get to know every secret, hidden thought, every hidden motive, every thought arising, without distortion – without saying of them that they are right, wrong, good or bad. *
Krishnamurti, *Krishnamurti on Education*

When a thought arises, do not judge it (remain a giraffe with your full awareness on the thought, keeping your jackal at bay). Merely observe it, as soon as a consciousness dawns in you that is actively involved in considering every kind of thought, every sort of feeling (this is giraffe consciousness). In this way, you can get to know every secret, hidden thought, every hidden motive, every thought arising, without distortion (without jackal interpretations) – without saying of them that they are right, wrong, good or bad (without jackal labels).

As a child, I was born with the tendency to watch people. Very consciously. I was really genuinely able to do it with my full attention. If I became intrigued by some character in the town, I'd sometimes follow him for streets at a time to study exactly how he walked. Every gesture, every facial expression was greedily absorbed, and when I got home, I'd do an imitation of him.
Toon Hermans (Dutch cabaret artist and poet), *Verhalen uit mijn Leven (Stories from my Life)*

Toon Hermans here describes how intensely his inner giraffe used to observe. He immersed himself so completely, physically too, that he as it were became the person he was observing. In my experience of him, there was always a loving respect in the manner in which he brought his characters to the stage, without the ridicule and criticism of the jackal.

Hardening ourselves is arming ourselves against all sorts of painful, unjust or unpleasant experiences. This suit of armor makes us, as it were, invulnerable, untouchable and without feeling, so we no longer feel these injustices and so on.

We no longer need this self-protection once we have learned to create a place of inner peace within ourselves, which cannot be swayed by any emotion, hurt or pain from without. We can then greet life from this inner core of peace and trust.

Hans Stolp, *De Geboorte van Christus in ons (The Birth of Christ in us)*

Hardening ourselves is arming ourselves against all sorts of painful, unjust or unpleasant experiences. This suit of armor makes us as it were, invulnerable, untouchable and without feeling, so we no longer feel these injustices and so on (a jackal, isolating himself; he connects neither with the outer world nor with his own inner world).

We no longer need this self-protection once we have learned to create a place of inner peace within ourselves, which cannot be swayed by any emotion, hurt or pain from without. We can then greet life from this inner core of peace and trust (the giraffe, making contact with the peace within and from there, connecting with the exterior world).

To the inferior eye, all else is superior: others are cleverer, more brilliant and talented than you.

To the loving eye, all is real. This form of love is neither sentimental nor naïve. A love such as this is the most important criterion for truth, praise and reality.

The loving eye can tempt even pain, hurt and violence into change and renewal. Full of love, it can witness all things. *

John O'Donohue, *Anam Cara, A Book of Celtic Wisdom*

I have written about jackal and giraffe ears. This is about jackal and giraffe eyes. The former watch and compare, while the latter watch reality with love. And the giraffe supports the jackal in his process of transformation.

When differences of opinion are seen as grounds for conflict, there is discussion or debate, but no dialogue. 'Being different' is then seen as a boundary, which is then guarded as a dividing line. This happens when people connect judgments of good and bad to the differences. As soon as boundaries are seen as meeting places with the power to connect and unify, there is an inspiring atmosphere in which love triumphs.

Marieke de Vrij, *Dialoog, de Wezenlijke Weg (Dialogue, the Essential Way)*

To a jackal, boundaries are lines of division. To giraffes, they are meeting places where you can touch one another.

'I don't want to bicker,' I said. 'I don't want to argue with you.'
'How do you know?' she said softly. 'How do you know it isn't the only way you can learn some lessons? If you didn't need to fight to learn things, you wouldn't cause so many problems! Sometimes I only understand you when you get angry.'
I blinked my eyes and looked at her in shock. 'Are you trying to say that everything's perfect? That our rows bring about an understanding that wasn't there to begin with?' *

Richard Bach, *The Bridge Across Forever*

The narrator wants harmony and imagines he will fulfill this need by avoiding an argument. She explains to him how important it is to allow his jackal to speak. That by listening to his jackal with giraffe ears, she can understand what is bothering him and what his needs are. That, once his jackal has had his say, his giraffe is able to listen to her and can understand her.

And finally, a piece by an unknown author.

Once there was a wise woman. On her journey through the mountains, she found a precious stone in a stream. The next day, she met another traveler who was hungry and she opened her bag in order to share her food with him. The hungry traveler saw the stone and asked her to give it to him. Without hesitation, she gave him the stone. The traveler departed, pleased at his good luck. He knew the stone was so valuable that he would not have a worry in the world for the rest of his life. But a few days later, he came back to return the stone to the woman. "I have been thinking," he said, "I know how much this stone is worth, but I am returning it to you in the hope that you will be able to give me something far more valuable. I would like you to give me that quality in you which allowed you to give it to me."

The man in the story is at first in his jackal, he is out to profit himself. He later returns to exchange the precious stone for the miracle of the giraffe.

As you can see, I often think I can recognize my two friends in what I read. My mind is on them so much of the time that I have grown to enjoy collecting them. Amongst other things, I have giraffe mugs and a teapot, a giraffe letter-opener, giraffe figurines and lots of cards with giraffes on them. What I miss are the jackals. The idea of appreciating our inner jackals has apparently not yet occurred to the manufacturers who make these things. I think it would be fantastic if little sets were to come onto the market: salt and pepper sets, book-ends, stationery, you name it. To remind us to embrace both the giraffe and the jackal within.

---

*   Translator's note: The passages quoted in this chapter have all been translated from the Dutch versions used in Justine's original. Previously existing English versions have not been used here.

Male giraffes sometimes fight over a female. They 'joust' as it were, with their necks. For these purposes, they choose a male with approximately the same strength, so they are a good match for each other. It is as if they respect the weakness of some of their species. They test their powers within the bounds of good sportsmanship.

We can use this as a metaphor for the competitive element in mankind. When we are in competition, we can stay in connection with each other as long as everyone involved is taking part voluntarily and as long as we treat our opponents with respect.

The idea that the jackal is a mean, aggressive animal comes from the past. The following describes how they really are. Jackals live on their own or in pairs. They sometimes form small groups. They are one of the few mammal species whereby the male and female form a relationship for life. Research shows that jackals are flexible hunters who cooperate with each other. They are also able to adapt to changing environments.

Jackals have long had the reputation of being sly and crafty. In human terms, we could say people thought they were manipulators. I would like to express my respect for the jackal as an animal and to thank the jackal's spirit for providing us with a symbol for a side of humanity in need of transformation.

Afterword

You may find that reading this book has activated the giraffe and the jackal in you. That you find yourself continually seeing and hearing giraffe and jackal snouts and ears. If I have managed to convey the following central ideas on the giraffe and the jackal, I will be deeply happy.

For a peaceful society, it is of essential importance that our inner giraffe accepts the jackal and gives him room for self- expression; that the giraffe hears the jackal's message and translates it into unfulfilled needs.

Of course, I also think it's important that we take respon-sibility for our own needs and make a contribution to the needs of others. Another thing I think is important... Whoa! Stop! I don't want to get repetitive.

Questions I am often asked are: 'Aren't those hand-puppets really meant for children?' 'Do you teach children too?' I understand these questions. But there is a little bit more to working with hand-puppets while wearing jackal or giraffe ears on your head than to watching a cartoon film or read-ing a children's book. My experience has been that some people find these props to be valuable additional tools in the learning process and get genuine pleasure from them, while others don't relate to them at all.

One question which preoccupies me is: 'Do I actually want to make children aware of how they communicate or could communicate, whether using the giraffe and jackal or not?' I examine this question by being open to the various opinions there are worldwide about teaching nonviolent communication to children whether explicitly or otherwise and the use of puppets thereby. Marshall Rosenberg says his experience is that children pick up the giraffe attitude much more quickly than adults do. Children are closer to their natural giraffe than we are. If we remind them, it's the most natural thing in the world to respond to a teacher who says: 'How can you be so stupid!' with: 'Am I doing something different from what you wanted me to do?' Marshall's advice to children is never to allow adults or structures to tempt them into either submission or rebellion.

In Israel, I have visited schools working in their own way with nonviolent communication. There are several giraffe schools in Israel. The parents and teachers are given training in NVC and the children are thus 'infected'. Each class has a giraffe corner where the children can get in touch with their feelings and needs in peace and where they can write giraffe messages and hang them up. Israeli and Palestinian schools working in this way are in contact with each other, organizing joint activities and inspiring one another.

I visited a school in Sweden working according to the principles of nonviolent communication. Marianne Göthlin, the school's foundress refers to it as a 'school based on needs'. The parents and teachers school themselves constantly in this form of communication. The lesson plans, the school timetable, the way the classroom is arranged, interaction with the children, everything is permeated with it. No mention is made of giraffes or jackals until the children are about 12. I was allowed to observe a handicrafts lesson. There was one little boy who went and sat on the sofa in a little side room with a book. This room is there especially for children who want to withdraw for a bit. At a certain point, there was an argument because there were other children who wanted to sit in the room too. The little boy was bothered by their talking and rough-and-tumble. The teacher went over to them. She asked the children some questions and reflected back to them the feelings and needs she thought they had. She asked them to think of a solution that was agreeable to everyone. She made no accusations, gave no punishment. When peace was restored, she returned to the class. The children at this school are encouraged to deal with confrontations in this way and to mediate in conflicts themselves.

A number of schools in Serbia work with a program called 'Words are Windows or they're Walls'. There are lessons for the various age-groups enabling the children, with the help of their teachers, to become familiar with nonviolent communication. There, they use the snake instead of the jackal.

There are activities being undertaken in schools in other countries too, such as Australia, Italy, Germany and the United States. Various books have also been written on the subject, amongst others by Marshall Rosenberg. For further information on nonviolent communication and children, you can go to www.cnvc.org . You may find some inspiration on the subject of raising children without punishment or rewards in my book 'Growing up in Trust'.

I myself work mainly with adults who wish to raise their consciousness and want to apply nonviolent communication in their own lives. Some of these people have children or work with children and want to convey this way of communicating to these children. They do this by setting an example themselves or by finding their own way (with or without giraffes and jackals) of presenting these ideas.

I also work with families, parents and children and then we use the hand-puppets.
I am somewhat reticent about teaching children giraffe language if their parents and other adults in their environment are continuing to relate to them in the old and trusted ways. Is it not perhaps more fruitful if parents and teach-

ers set the example and if children absorb it through their natural tendency to imitate? Beside this, you can go as far as you like in actively presenting lessons and lesson material around this subject and I hope this book may inspire you to develop both.

In Munich, Germany they work with the 'Giraffentraum', a programme for pre-schoolers using stories about a little giraffe who has lost his mother, which leads the children through the steps in the model of nonviolent communication. The jackal does not appear in this programme. I have talked to the developers of this programme, Frank and Gundi Gaschler. The idea behind working with the giraffe and not the jackal is to give attention only to what you want to stimulate. They clothe the message about the giraffe in a story.

Whether you want to get to know and learn to value the giraffe and the jackal at home or at work, on holiday or while you're doing the shopping, within your club or political party: I hope first and foremost, that you have fun with them!

About the author

Justine Mol (1949) was born in a Dutch catholic family. She was the seventh child out of ten. She raised three children of her own.

In 1999 she read an article on Nonviolent Communication by Marshall Rosenberg. In September 2004 she was certified as an international NVC trainer. After a few years she withdrew from the international network. In the course of these years she started writing articles on NVC and the Raising of Children. She also translated two books into Dutch: *The Inside Story*, Understanding the Power of Feelings, and *Teaching Children to Love* by Doc Lew Childre, both books published by the Institute of Heart Math in California.

After *Growing up in Trust* she wrote T*he giraffe and the jackal in us (2007).* Her books *Geweldig Communiceren met Jonge Mensen, Geweldig Communiceren voor Jonge Mensen* and *Ik werd overvallen* have not yet been published in English. On the last book you can find an interview on her website www.justinemol.nl in which she tells how she reacted nonviolently to an assault in her house on November 2011.
Besides writing she gives trainings and lectures on her books and on NVC in the Netherlands and abroad, guides people through personal processes in individual coaching. In May 2008 she finished a training in Zen Coaching with Kåre Landfald from Norway.

Since 2006 she supports Henk Haalboom, a man who was found guilty for a murder that most probably never took place. Haalboom has been in prison since January 2002. There is a website from his support group *Hart voor Henk*

Haalboom, www.onschuldiggevangen.nl. Part of it is in English.

Bibliography

D'Ansembourg, Thomas – Being Genuine: Stop Being Nice, Start Being Real - Puddle Dancer Press

Bach, Richard – The Bridge Across Forever – Dell Publishing

Chopra, Deepak – Peace is the Way

Guilmartin, Nance – Healing Conversations: What to Say When You Don't Know What to Say – Jossey-Bass

Hermans, Toon – Verhalen uit mijn Leven (Stories from my Life) – Fontein

Katie, Byron – Loving What is: Four Questions That Can Change Your Life – Harmony Books

Krishnamurti, J. – Krishnamurti on Education – Orient Longman Ltd.

Krishnamurti, J. – A Wholly Different Way of Living – KFI

Martin, William – The Parent's Tao Te Ching

McTaggart, Lynne – The Field – Harper Collins

Mol, Justine – Growing up in Trust – O Books

O'Donohue, John – Aman Cara: A Book of Celtic Wisdom – Harper Collins

Oriah Mountain Dreamer – The Invitation – HarperSanFrancisco

Rosenberg, Marshall – Nonviolent Communication – Puddle Dancer Press

Stolp, Hans – De Geboorte van Christus in ons (The Birth of Christ in us) – Ankh Hermes

De Vrij, Marieke – Dialoog (Dialogue) – De Vrije Mare

Williamson, Marianne – The Gift of Change

Websites

Justine Mol, www.justinemol.nl

Center for Nonviolent Communication, www.cnvc.org

Colophon

The Giraffe and Jackal Within
About Nonviolent Communication
Justine Mol

ISBN 978 90 8850 373 3
NUR 847

Translation
Dawn Mastin

Illustrations
Sjeng Schupp

Design Cover
Lieve Maas

Layout and typesetting
Merel van Dam, SWP Publishers

Publisher
Trude van Waarden

For information on other SWP publications:
P.O.Box 257, 1000 AG Amsterdam
Tel.: + 31 (0)20 330 72 00
E-mail: swp@mailswp.com
Internet: www.swpbook.com

Lightning Source UK Ltd.
Milton Keynes UK
UKHW011202271218
334616UK00024B/494/P

9 789088 503733